LUST, CAUTION

LUST, CAUTION

The Story, the Screenplay, and the Making of the Film

STORY BY *Eileen Chang*

SCREENPLAY BY *Wang Hui Ling*
AND *James Schamus*

PREFACE BY *Ang Lee*

PANTHEON BOOKS

New York

Afterword, notes on names, and translation of "Lust, Caution"
copyright © 2007 by Julia Lovell
Text and photographs copyright © 2007 by Mr. Yee
Productions, LLC
Screenplay of *Lust, Caution* copyright © 2007 by Mr. Yee
Productions, LLC

"Lust, Caution" was originally published in Taiwan as "Se Jie" in
Wangran Ji by Eileen Chang, published by Crown Publishing
Company Ltd., Taipei, in 1983. Copyright © 1983 by Eileen Chang.

Library of Congress Cataloging-in-Publication Data
Zhang, Ailing.
Lust, caution : the story, the screenplay, and the making of the film /
story by Eileen Chang / screenplay by James Schamus and
Wang Hui Ling ; preface by Ang Lee.
p. cm.
Includes bibliographical references.
ISBN-13: 978-0-375-42524-0
1. Se jie (Motion picture) I. Schamus, James, 1959–
II. Wang, Huiling, 1964– III. Title.
PN1997.2.S4Z43 2007
791.43'72—dc22
2007021256

www.pantheonbooks.com

Printed in the United States of America

First Edition

2 4 6 8 9 7 5 3 1

CONTENTS

Contents

PREFACE

Ang Lee

To me, no writer has ever used the Chinese language as cruelly as Zhang Ailing (Eileen Chang), and no story of hers is as beautiful or as cruel as "Lust, Caution." She revised the story for years and years—for decades—returning to it as a criminal might return to the scene of a crime, or as a victim might reenact a trauma, reaching for pleasure only by varying and reimagining the pain. Making our film, we didn't really "adapt" Zhang's work, we simply kept returning to her theater of cruelty and love until we had enough to make a movie of it.

Zhang is very specific in the traps her words set. For example, in Chinese we have the figure of the tiger who kills a person. Thereafter, the person's ghost willingly works for the tiger, helping to lure more prey into the jungle. The Chinese phrase for this is *wei hu dzuo chung.* It's a common phrase and was often used to refer to the Chinese who collaborated with the Japanese occupiers during the war. In the story Zhang has Yee allude to this phrase to describe the relationship between men and women. Alive, Chia-chih was his woman; dead, she is his ghost, his *chung*. But perhaps she already was one when they first met, and now, from beyond her grave, she is luring him closer to the tiger. . . .

Interestingly, the word for *tiger's ghost* sounds exactly like the word for *prostitute*. So in the movie, in the Japanese tavern scene, Yee refers to himself with this word. It could refer to his relationship to the Japanese — he is both their whore and their *chung*. But it also means he knows he is already a dead man.

We, the readers of Zhang Ailing, are we her *chung*? Often the transition from one life into the next is made unexpectedly, as an experience of the imagination. Zhang describes the feeling Chia-chih had after performing on stage as a young woman, the rush she felt afterward, that she could barely calm down even after a late-night meal with her friends from the theater and a ride on the upper deck of a tram. When I read that, my mind raced back to my own first experience on the stage, back in 1973 at the Academy of Art in Taipei: the same rush of energy at the end of the play, the same late-night camaraderie, the same wandering. I realized how that experience was central to Zhang's work, and how it could be transformed into film. She understood playacting and mimicry as something by nature cruel and brutal: animals, like her characters, use camouflage to evade their enemies and lure their prey. But mimicry and performance are also ways we open ourselves as human beings to greater experience, indefinable connections to others, higher meanings, art, and the truth.

INTRODUCTION

James Schamus

Why did she do it?

The question is itself an admission of the impossibility of ever really answering it.

And yet we ask.

Another, more specific, way of asking:

What act, exactly, does Wang Chia-chih perform at that fateful moment in the jeweler's shop when she decides whether or not to go through with the murder of her lover?

And here, two words—*act* and *perform*—indicate the troubling question Zhang Ailing (Eileen Chang) asks us: for at the crucial moment when we *choose*, when we *decide*, when we *exercise our free will*, are we not also *performing*?

One could say that "Lust, Caution" depicts a heroine who "becomes herself" only when she takes on the identity of another, for only behind the mask of the character Mai Tai-tai can Chia-chih truly desire, and thus truly live—playacting allows her to discover her one real love. But this is too reductive. For the performer always, by definition, performs *for* someone. And that audience, no matter how entranced, is always complicit: it knows deep down that the performance isn't real, but it also knows the cathartic truth the performer strives for is attainable only when that truth is, indeed, *performed*. Yee doesn't simply desire Mai Tai-tai while suspecting she is not who she says she is; it is precisely *because* he suspects her that he desires her. In this sense his desire is the same as hers: he wants to *know* her. And so lust and caution are, in Zhang's work, functions of each other, not because we desire what is dangerous, but because our love is, no matter how earnest, an *act*, and therefore always an object of suspicion.

If Chia-chih's act at the end of the story is indeed an expression of love, it paradoxically destroys the very theatrical contract that made the performance of that love possible — in killing off her fictional character, she effectively kills herself. Her act is thus a negation of the very idea that it could be acknowledged, understood, explained, or reciprocated by its audience.[1]

---

[1] I get much of this sense of the "act" from the philosopher Slavoj Žižek. See his *Enjoy Your Symptom!: Jacques Lacan in Hollywood and Out* (New York: Routledge, 2001): "The act differs from an active intervention (action) in that it radically transforms its bearer (agent): the act is not simply something

I think one of the things that drew Ang Lee, and the rest of us with him, toward Zhang Ailing's work was a feeling that her writing itself is just this kind of "act"—a profound cry of protest against the warring structures of domination that so cataclysmically shaped midcentury China and made her life a long series of displacements. "Lust, Caution" is of course not a work of autobiography, but in it we see the shape of Zhang's life, and its terrible disorientations, ghosted behind almost every line.

Like her heroine, Wang Chia-chih, Zhang was a student in Hong Kong during the Pacific War's early years; the Japanese invasion of Hong Kong in 1941 cut short her English studies at the University of Hong Kong, precipitating her return to her aunt and mother's home in Shanghai—a home to which she had fled a few years earlier after a stay with her opium-addicted, abusive father. In Shanghai she married her first husband, a philanderer who served in the collaborationist government; when the Japanese were defeated, he fled and took up with another woman. Like

---

that I 'accomplish'—after an act, I'm literally 'not the same as before' . . . in it, the subject is annihilated and subsequently reborn (or not) . . ." (p. 44). For Žižek, the act is a supreme form of feminine rejection: "we shouldn't forget that the paradigmatic case of such an act is feminine: Antigone's 'No!' to Creon, to state power; her act is literally suicidal, she excludes herself from the community, whereby she offers nothing new, no positive program—she just insists on her unconditional demand" (p. 46).

Chia-chih, Zhang had earlier tried to get to London, but the war eclipsed those plans, too. In 1952, she moved to Hong Kong, and from there to the United States, where she died, in 1995, at the age of seventy-five, in Los Angeles. A precocious and accomplished literary genius, she wrote masterpieces in her early twenties. She continued to write, both in Chinese and English, into the 1970s, and though her works were banned for a long time in Mainland China, she has remained a revered and widely read author throughout the Chinese-speaking world.

Zhang did not just transmute her private sagas into art; she took the dominant cultural and political myths of her day and followed her characters to their bitterest ends as they fulfilled those myths. In this, she made use in particular of another "Shanghai Xiaoxie" (Shanghai Miss) of the 1920s and '30s, a woman who was perhaps the greatest star the Chinese cinema has ever produced: Ruan Lingyu. Ruan, even in her day, was something of a mythic figure, revered with an uncommon fervor—it is said, for example, that at her funeral in 1935 the procession was more than two miles long. Facing a public scandal caused by a ne'er-do-well former lover, she killed herself at the age of twenty-five. Her death was a national trauma, made all the more disturbing by the fact that in her last film, the wildly popular *New Woman* (1935, directed by Cai Chu-sheng), she portrayed a character who also met her death at her own hand—a character based on a real actress, Ai Xia, who had herself committed suicide.[2] Wang Chia-chih, like Ruan Lingyu, is a woman caught up in a game of cinematic and literary mirrors, a game that has now ensnared Ang Lee as he reflects his own cinematic mirror onto Zhang Ailing's remarkable work.

---

[2] See Zhang Zhen, *An Amorous History of the Silver Screen: Shanghai Cinema 1896–1937* (Chicago: University of Chicago Press, 2005), p. 266. The Hong Kong filmmaker Stanley Kwan has made a remarkable film about Ruan Lingyu, titled *Center Stage* (1992).

LUST, CAUTION

A Story by Eileen Chang

Though it was still daylight, the hot lamp was shining full-beam over the mahjong table. Diamond rings flashed under its glare as their wearers clacked and reshuffled their tiles. The tablecloth, tied down over the table legs, stretched out into a sleek plain of blinding white. The harsh artificial light silhouetted to full advantage the generous curve of Chia-chih's bosom, and laid bare the elegant lines of her hexagonal face, its beauty somehow accentuated by the imperfectly narrow forehead, by the careless, framing wisps of hair. Her makeup was understated, except for the glossily rouged arcs of her lips. Her hair she had pinned nonchalantly back from her face, then allowed to hang down to her shoulders. Her sleeveless cheongsam of electric blue moiré satin reached to the knees, its shallow, rounded collar standing only half an inch tall, in the Western style. A brooch fixed to the collar matched her diamond-studded sapphire button earrings.

The two ladies — *Tai-tais* — immediately to her left and right were both wearing black wool capes, each held fast at the neck by a heavy double gold chain that snaked out from beneath the cloak's turned-down collar. Isolated from the rest of the world by Japanese occupation, Shanghai had elaborated a few native fashions. Thanks to the extravagantly inflated price of gold in the occupied territories, gold chains as thick as these were now fabulously expensive. But somehow, functionally worn in place of a collar button, they managed to avoid the taint of vulgar ostentation, thereby offering their owners the perfect pretext for parading their wealth on excursions about the city. For these excellent reasons, the cape and gold chain had become the favored uniform of the wives of officials serving in Wang Ching-wei's puppet government. Or perhaps they were following the lead of Chungking, the Chinese Nationalist regime's wartime capital, where black cloaks were very much in vogue among the elegant ladies of the political glitterati.

Yee Tai-tai was *chez elle*, so she had dispensed with her own cape; but even without it, her figure still seemed to bell outward from her neck, with all the weight the years had put on her. She'd met Chia-chih two years earlier in Hong Kong,

after she and her husband had left Chungking —
and the Nationalist government — together with
Wang Ching-wei. Not long before the couple took
refuge on the island, one of Wang Ching-wei's
lieutenants, Cheng Chung-ming, had been assassinated in Hanoi, and so Wang's followers in
Hong Kong were keeping their heads down.
Yee Tai-tai, nonetheless, was determined to go
shopping. During the war, goods were scarce in
both the unconquered interior and the occupied
territories of the Mainland; Yee Tai-tai had no
intention of wasting the golden purchasing opportunity offered by a stopover in the commercial
paradise of Hong Kong. Someone in her circle
introduced her to Chia-chih — the beautiful young
wife of Mr. Mai, a local businessman — who
chaperoned her on her shopping trips. If you
wanted to navigate Hong Kong's emporiums, you
had to have a local along: you were expected to
haggle over prices even in the biggest department
stores, and if you couldn't speak Cantonese, all
the traders would overcharge you wickedly. Mr.
Mai was in import-export and, like all business-
people, delighted in making political friends. So
of course the couple were incessantly hospitable
to Yee Tai-tai, who was in turn extremely grate-
ful. After the bombing of Pearl Harbor and the
fall of Hong Kong, Mr. Mai went out of business.
To make some extra money for the family, Mai
Tai-tai decided to do a little smuggling herself,

and traveled to Shanghai with a few luxury goods—watches, Western medicines, perfumes, stockings—to sell. Yee Tai-tai very naturally invited her to stay with them.

"We went to Shu-yü, that Szechuanese restaurant, yesterday," Yee Tai-tai was telling the first black cape. "Mai Tai-tai hadn't been."

"Oh, really?"

"We haven't seen you here for a few days, Ma Tai-tai."

"I've been busy—a family matter," Ma Tai-tai mumbled amid the twittering of the mahjong tiles.

Yee Tai-tai's lips thinned into a smile. "She went into hiding because it was her turn to buy dinner."

Chia-chih suspected that Ma Tai-tai was jealous. Ever since Chia-chih had arrived, she had been the center of attention.

"Liao Tai-tai took us all out last night. She's been on such a winning streak the last couple of days," Yee Tai-tai went on to Ma Tai-tai. "At the restaurant, I bumped into that young Mr. Lee and his wife and invited them to join us. When he said they were waiting for guests of their own, I told him they should all join us. After all, it isn't often that Liao Tai-tai gives dinner parties. Then it turned out Mr. Lee had invited so many guests we couldn't fit them all around our table. Even with extra chairs we couldn't all squeeze in, so Liao Tai-tai had to sit behind me like a singsong girl at a banquet. 'What a beauty I've picked for myself tonight,' I joked. 'I'm too old a piece of tofu for you to swallow,' she replied. 'Old tofu tastes the spiciest,' I told her! Oh, how we laughed. She laughed so much her pockmarks turned red."

More laughter around the mahjong table.

While Yee Tai-tai was still updating Ma Tai-tai on the goings-on of the past couple of days, Mr. Yee came in, dressed in a gray suit, and nodded at his three female guests.

"You started early today."

He stood behind his wife, watching the game. The wall behind him was swathed in heavy yellowish-brown wool curtains printed with a brick-red phoenix-tail fern design, each blade almost six feet long. Chou Fo-hai, Wang Ching-wei's second in command, had a pair; and so, therefore, did they. False french windows, and enormous drapes to cover them, were all the rage just then. Because of the war, fabrics were in short supply; floor-length curtains such as those hanging behind Mr. Yee—using up an entire bolt of cloth, with extra wastage from pattern matching—were a conspicuous extravagance. Standing against the huge ferns of his backdrop, Yee looked even shorter than usual. His face was pale, finely drawn, and crowned by a receding hairline that faded away into petal-shaped peaks above his temples. His nose was distinguished by its narrowed, almost ratlike tip.

"Is that ring of yours three carats, Ma Tai-tai?"

Yee Tai-tai asked. "The day before yesterday, P'in Fen brought a five-carat diamond to show me, but it didn't sparkle like yours."

"I've heard P'in Fen's things are better than the stuff in the shops."

"It is convenient to have things brought to your home, I suppose. And you can hold on to them for a few days, while you decide. And sometimes she has things you can't get elsewhere. Last time, she showed me a yellow kerosene diamond, but *he* wouldn't buy it." She glanced icily at Mr. Yee before going on: "How much do you imagine something like that would cost now? A perfect kerosene diamond: a dozen ounces of gold per carat? Two? Three? P'in Fen says no one's selling kerosene or pink diamonds at the moment, for any price. Everyone's hoarding them, waiting for the price to get even more insane."

"Didn't you feel how heavy it was?" Mr. Yee laughed. "Ten carats. You wouldn't have been able to play mahjong with that rock on your finger."

The edges of the table glittered like a diamond exhibition, Chia-chih thought, every pair of hands glinting ostentatiously—except hers. She should have left her jadeite ring back in its box, she realized; to spare herself all those sneering glances.

"Stop making fun of me!" Yee Tai-tai sulked as she moved out one of her counters. The black cape opposite Ma Tai-tai clatteringly opened out her winning hand, and a sudden commotion of laughter and lament broke the thread of conversation.

As the gamblers busily set to calculating their wins and losses, Mr. Yee motioned slightly at Chia-chih with his chin toward the door.

She immediately glanced at the two black capes on either side of her. Fortunately, neither seemed to have noticed. She paid out the chips she had lost, took a sip from her teacup, then suddenly exclaimed: "That memory of mine! I have a business appointment at three o'clock, I'd forgotten all about it. Mr. Yee, will you take my place until I get back?"

"I won't allow it!" Yee Tai-tai protested. "You can't just run away like that without warning us in advance."

"And just when I thought my luck was changing," muttered the winning black cape.

"I suppose we could ask Liao Tai-tai to come over. Go and telephone her," Yee Tai-tai went on to Chia-chih. "At least stay until she gets here."

"I really need to go now." Chia-chih looked at her watch. "I'm going to be late — I arranged to have coffee with a broker. Mr. Yee can take my place."

"I'm busy this afternoon," Mr. Yee excused himself. "Tomorrow I'll play all night."

"That Wang Chia-chih!" Yee Tai-tai liked referring to Chia-chih by her full maiden name, as if they had known each other since they were girls. "I'll make you pay for this—you're going to treat us all to dinner tonight!"

"You can't let your guest buy you dinner," Ma Tai-tai objected.

"I'm siding with Yee Tai-tai," the other black cape put in.

They needed to tread carefully around their hostess on the subject of her young houseguest. Although Yee Tai-tai was easily old enough to be Chia-chih's mother, there had never been any talk of formalizing their relationship, of adopting her as a goddaughter. Yee Tai-tai was a little unpredictable, at the age she was now. Although she had a dowager's fondness for keeping young, pretty women clustered around her—like a galaxy of stars reflecting glory onto the moon around which they circulated—she was not yet too old for flashes of feminine jealousy.

"All right, all right," Chia-chih said. "I'll take you all out to dinner tonight. But you won't be in the party, Mr. Yee, if you don't take my place now."

"Do, Mr. Yee! Mahjong's no fun with only three. Play just for a little, while Ma Tai-tai telephones for a replacement."

"I really do have a prior engagement." Whenever Mr. Yee spoke of official business, his voice sank to an almost inaudibly discreet mutter. "Someone else will come along soon."

"We all know how busy Mr. Yee is," Ma Tai-
tai said.

Was she insinuating something, Chia-chih
wondered, or were nerves getting the better of
her? Observing him smile and banter, Chia-chih
even began to read a flattering undertone into
Ma Tai-tai's remark, as if she knew that he wanted
other people to coax the details of his con-
quest out of him. Perhaps success, she speculated,
can turn the heads of even the professionally
secretive.

It was getting far too dangerous. If the job
wasn't done today, if the thing were to drag on any
longer, Yee Tai-tai would surely find them out.

He walked off while she was still exhaustingly
negotiating her exit with his wife. After finally
extricating herself, she returned briefly to her
room. As she finished hurriedly tidying her hair
and makeup—there was too little time to change
her clothes—the maidservant arrived to tell her
the car was waiting for her at the door. Getting
in, she gave the chauffeur instructions to drive
her to a café; once arrived, she sent him back
home.

As it was only midafternoon, the café was
almost deserted. Its large interior was lit by wall
lamps with pleated apricot silk shades, its floor
populated by small round tables covered in cloths
of fine white linen jacquard—an old-fashioned,

11

middlebrow kind of establishment. She made a call from the public telephone on the counter. After four rings, she hung up and redialed, muttering "wrong number" to herself, for fear the cashier might think her behavior strange.

That was the code. The second time, someone answered.

"Hello?"

Thank goodness—it was K'uang Yu-min. Even now, she was terrified she might have to speak to Liang Jun-sheng, though he was usually very careful to let others get to the phone first.

"It's me," she replied in Cantonese. "Everyone well?"

"All fine. How about yourself?"

"I'll be going shopping this afternoon, but I'm not sure when."

"No problem. We'll wait for you. Where are you now?"

"Hsia-fei Road."

"Fine."

A pause.

"Nothing else then?" Her hands felt cold, but she was somehow warmed by the sound of a familiar voice.

"No, nothing."

"I might go there right now."

"We'll be there, don't worry. See you later."

She hung up and exited to hail a pedicab.

If they didn't finish it off today, she couldn't

stay on at the Yees'—not with all those great bejeweled cats watching her every move. Maybe she should have found an excuse to move out as soon as she had hooked him. He could have found her a place somewhere: the last couple of times they'd met in apartments, different ones each time, left vacant by British or Americans departed to war camps. But that probably would have made everything even more complicated—how would she have known what time he was coming? He might have suddenly descended upon her at any moment. Or if they had fixed a time in advance, urgent business might have forced him to cancel at the last minute. Calling him would also have been difficult, as his wife kept a close eye on him; she probably had spies stationed in all his various offices. A hint of suspicion and the whole thing would be undone: Shanghai crawled with potential informers, all of them eager to ingratiate themselves with the mighty Yee Tai-tai. And if Chia-chih had not pursued him so energetically, he might have cast her aside. Apartments were a popular parting gift to discarded mistresses of Wang Ching-wei's ministers. He had too many temptations jostling before him; far too many for any one moment. And if one of them weren't kept constantly in view, it would slip to the back of his mind and out of sight. No: he had to be nailed—even if she had to keep his nose buried between her breasts to do it.

"They weren't this big two years ago," he had murmured to her, in between kisses.

His head against her chest, he hadn't seen her blush.

Even now, it stung her to recall those knowing smirks—from all of them, K'uang Yu-min included. Only Liang Jun-sheng had pretended not to notice how much bigger her breasts now looked. Some episodes from her past she needed to keep banished from her mind.

It was some distance to the foreign concessions. When the pedicab reached the corner of Ching-an Temple and Seymour roads, she told him to stop by a small café. She looked around her, on the off chance that his car had already arrived. She could see only a vehicle with a bulky charcoal-burning tank parked a little way up the street.

Most of the café's business must have been in takeout; there were hardly any places to sit down inside. Toward the back of its dingy interior was a refrigerated cabinet filled with various Western-style cakes. A glaringly bright lamp in the passage-way behind exposed the rough, uneven surface of the brown paint covering the lower half of the walls. A white military-style uniform hung to one side of a small fridge; above, nearer the ceiling, hung a row of long, lined gowns—like a rail in a secondhand clothing store—worn by the estab-lishment's Chinese servants and waiters.

He had told her that the place had been

opened by a Chinese who had started out working in Tientsin's oldest, most famous Western
eatery, the Kiessling. He must have chosen this
place, she thought, because he would be unlikely
to run into any high-society acquaintances here.
It was also situated on a main road, so if he did
bump into someone, it would not look as suspicious as if he were seen somewhere off the
beaten track; it was central enough that one could
plausibly be on one's way to somewhere entirely
aboveboard.

She waited, the cup of coffee in front of her
steadily losing heat. The last time, in the apartment, he had kept her waiting almost a whole
hour. If the Chinese are the most unpunctual of
people, she meditated, their politicians are surely
virtuosos in the art of the late arrival. If she had
to wait much longer, the store would be closed
before they got there.

It had been his idea in the first place, after their
first assignation. "Let's buy you a ring to celebrate
today—you choose it. I'd go with you myself, if I
had the time." Their second meeting was an even
more rushed affair, and he had not mentioned it
again. If he failed to remember today, she would
have to think of artful ways of reminding him.
With any other man, she would have made herself
look undignified, grasping. But a cynical old fox
like him would not delude himself that a pretty
young woman would attach herself to a squat fifty-

year-old merely for the beauty of his soul; a failure to express her material interest in the affair would seem suspicious. Ladies, in any case, are always partial to jewelry. She had, supposedly, traveled to Shanghai to trade in feminine luxuries. That she should try to generate a little extra profit along the way was entirely to be expected. As he was in the espionage business himself, he probably suspected conspiracies even where they didn't exist, where no cause for doubt had been given. Her priority was to win his trust, to appear credible. So far they had met in locations of his choosing; today she had to persuade him to follow her lead.

Last time he had sent the car on time to fetch her. The long wait she had had to endure today must mean he was coming himself. That was a relief: if they were due to tryst in an apartment, it would be hard to coax him out again once they were ensconced. Unless he had planned for them to stay out late together, to go out somewhere for dinner first—but he hadn't taken her to dinner on either of the previous two occasions. He would be wanting to take his time with her, while she would be getting jittery that the shop would close; but she wouldn't be able to hurry him along, like a prostitute with a customer.

She took out her powder compact and dabbed at her face. There was no guarantee he'd be coming to meet her himself. Now that the novelty had

worn off, he was probably starting to lose interest. If she didn't pull it off today, she might not get
another chance.

She glanced at her watch again. She felt a kind
of chilling premonition of failure, like a long snag
in a silk stocking, silently creeping up her body.
On a seat a little over the way from hers, a man
dressed in a Chinese robe — also on his own, reading a newspaper — was studying her. He'd been
there when she had arrived, so he couldn't have
been following her. Perhaps he was trying to
guess what line of business she was in; whether
her jewelry was real or fake. She didn't have the
look of a dancing girl, but if she was an actress, he
couldn't put a name to the face.

She had, in a past life, been an actress; and
here she was, still playing a part, but in a drama
too secret to make her famous.

While at college in Canton she'd starred in a
string of rousingly patriotic history plays. Before
the city fell to the Japanese, her university had
relocated to Hong Kong, where the drama troupe
had given one last public performance. Over-
excited, unable to wind down after the curtain had
fallen, she had gone out for a bite to eat with the
rest of the cast. But even after almost everyone else
had dispersed, she still hadn't wanted to go home.
Instead, she and two female classmates had ridden
through the city on the deserted upper deck of a

tram as it swayed and trundled down the middle of
the Hong Kong streets, the neon advertisements
glowing in the darkness outside the windows.

Hong Kong University had lent a few of its
classrooms to the Cantonese students, but lectures
were always jam-packed, uncomfortably reminding them of their refugee status. The disappointing
apathy of average Hong Kong people toward
China's state of national emergency filled the classmates with a strong, indignant sense of exile, even
though they had traveled little more than a hundred miles over the border to reach Hong Kong.
Soon enough, a few like-minded elements among
them formed a small radical group. When Wang
Ching-wei, soon to begin negotiating with the
Japanese over forming a collaborationist government back on the Mainland, arrived on the
island with his retinue of supporters—many of
them also from near Canton—the students discovered that one of his aides came from the same town
as K'uang Yu-min. Exploiting this coincidence,
K'uang sought him out and easily struck up a
friendship, in the process extracting from him various items of useful information about members of
Wang's group. After he had reported his findings
to his coconspirators, they resolved after much
discussion to set a honey trap for one Mr. Yee:
to seduce him, with the help of one of their female classmates, toward an assassin's bullet. First
she would befriend the wife, then move in on

the husband. But if she presented herself as a student—always the most militant members of the population—Yee Tai-tai would be instantly on her guard. Instead, the group decided to make her the young wife of a local businessman; that sounded unthreatening enough, particularly in Hong Kong, where men of commerce were almost always apolitical. Enter the female star of the college drama troupe.

Of the various members of the group, Huang Lei was the wealthiest—from family money—and he briskly raised the funds to build a front for the conspiracy: renting a house, hiring a car, borrowing costumes. And since he was the only one of them able to drive, he took the part of chauffeur. Ou-yang Ling-wen was cast as the businessman husband, Mr. Mai; K'uang Yu-min as a cousin of the family, chaperoning the lovely Mai Tai-tai on her first meeting with Yee Tai-tai. After taking K'uang and the obligingly talkative aide back home, the car then drove the two ladies on to the Central District, to go about their shopping alone.

She had seen Mr. Yee a few times, but only in passing. When they finally sat down in the same room together—the first time the Yees invited her to play mahjong with them—she could tell right away he was interested, despite his obvious attempts to be circumspect. Since the age of twelve or thirteen, she had been no stranger to the admiring male gaze. She knew the game. He was terrified of indiscretion, but at the same time finding his tediously quiet life in Hong Kong stifling. He didn't even dare drink, for fear the Wangs might summon him for duty at any moment. He and another member of the Wang clique had rented an old house together, inside which they remained cloistered, diverting themselves only with the occasional game of mahjong.

During the game, the conversation turned to the fabric Yee Tai-tai had bought to make suits for her husband. Chia-chih recommended a tailor who had done work for her in the past. "He'll be madly busy right now, with all the tourist trade, so it could take him a few months. But if Yee Tai-tai telephones me when Mr. Yee has a free moment, I'll take him. He'll get them done faster if he knows it's for a friend of mine." As she was going, she left her phone number on the table. While his wife was at the door, seeing Chia-chih out, Mr. Yee would surely have time to copy it down for himself. Then, over the next couple of days, he could find an opportunity to call her—during office hours, when Mr. Mai would be out at work. And they could take it from there.

That evening a light drizzle had been falling. Huang Lei drove her back home and they went back into the house together, where everybody was nervously waiting for news of the evening's triumph. Resplendent in the high-society costume in which she had performed so supremely, she wanted everyone to stay on to celebrate with her, to carouse with her until morning. None of the male students were dancers, but a bowl of soup at one of those small all-night restaurants and a long walk through the damp night would do just as well. Anything to avoid bed.

Instead, a quiet gradually fell over the assembled company. There was whispering in a couple of corners, and secretive, tittering laughter; laughter she had heard before. They had been talking it over behind her back for some time, she realized.

"Apparently, Liang Jun-sheng is the only one who has any experience," Lai Hsiu-chin, the only other girl in the group, told her.

Liang Jun-sheng.

Of course. He was the only one who had been inside a brothel.

But given that she had already determined to make a sacrifice of herself, she couldn't very well resent him for being the only candidate for the job.

And that evening, while she basked in the heady afterglow of her success, even Liang Jun-sheng didn't seem quite as repellent as usual. One by one, the others saw the way the thing would go; one by one they slipped away, until the two of them were left alone. And so the show went on.

Days passed. Mr. Yee did not call. In the end, she decided to telephone Yee Tai-tai, who sounded listless, offhand: she'd been too busy to go shopping in the last few days, but she'd give her another ring in a day or two.

Did Yee Tai-tai suspect something? Had she discovered her husband in possession of Chia-chih's phone number? Or had they had bad news from the Japanese? After two weeks tormented by worry, she finally received a jubilant phone call from Yee Tai-tai: to say good-bye. She was sorry they were in such a hurry that there'd be no time to meet before they left, but they would love to have her and her husband visit in Shanghai. They must come for a good long time, so they could all go on a trip to Nanking together. Wang Ching-wei's plan to go back to Nanking to form a government must have temporarily run aground, Chia-chih speculated, and forced them to lie low for a while.

Huang Lei was by now in serious trouble, up to his eyes in debt. And when his family cut off his allowance on hearing that he was cohabiting with a dancing girl in Hong Kong, the scheme's finances collapsed.

The thing with Liang Jun-sheng had been awkward from the start; and now that she was so obviously regretting the whole business, the rest of the group began to avoid her. No one would look her in the eye.

"I was an idiot," she said to herself, "such an idiot."

Had she been set up, she wondered, from the very beginning of this dead-end drama?

From this point on, she kept her distance not only from Liang Jun-sheng, but also from their entire little group. All the time she was with them, she felt they were eyeing her curiously—as if she were some kind of freak, or grotesque. After Pearl Harbor, the sea lanes reopened and all her classmates transferred to Shanghai. Although it, too, had been occupied by the Japanese, its colleges were still open; there was still an education (of sorts) to be had. She did not go with them, and did not try to find them when she got there herself.

For a long time, she agonized over whether she had caught something from Liang Jun-sheng.

Not long after reaching Shanghai, however, the students made contact with an underground worker called Wu—doubtless an alias—who, as soon as he heard about the high-ranking connection they had made, naturally encouraged them to pursue their scheme. And when they approached her, she resolved to do her duty and see the thing through.

In truth, every time she was with Yee she felt cleansed, as if by a scalding hot bath; for now everything she did was for the cause.

They must have posted someone to watch the entrance to the café, and alert everyone the instant his car drew up. When she'd arrived, she hadn't spotted anyone loitering about. The P'ing-an Theater directly opposite would have been an obvious choice, its corridor of pillars offering the perfect cover for a lookout. People were, in any case, always hanging around theater entrances; one could easily wait there without arousing suspicion. But it was a little too far away to identify clearly the occupant of a car parked on the other side of the road.

A delivery bike, apparently broken down, was parked by the entrance to a leather goods shop next door. Its owner—a man of around thirty, with a crew cut—was bent over the mechanism, trying to repair it. Though she couldn't see his face clearly, she was fairly sure he wasn't someone she had seen before. She somehow doubted the bike was the getaway vehicle. There were some things they didn't tell her, and some she didn't ask. But she had heard that members of her old group had been chosen for the job. Even with Wu's help and connections, though, they might not have been able to get hold of a car for afterward. If that car with a charcoal tank stayed where it was, parked just up from the café, it might turn out to be theirs. In which case it would be Huang Lei at the wheel. As she'd approached the café from behind the vehicle, she hadn't seen the driver.

She suspected that Wu didn't have much faith in them: he was probably afraid they were too inexperienced, that they'd get caught and fall to pieces in an interrogation, implicating other people in the process. Chia-chih was sure he was more than a one-man operation here in Shanghai, but he'd been K'uang Yu-min's only point of contact throughout.

He'd promised to let them join his network. Maybe this was their test.

"Before they fire, they get so close the gun's almost up against the body," K'uang Yu-min had once told her, smiling. "They don't shoot from a distance, like in the movies."

This had probably been an attempt to reassure her that they wouldn't cut everyone around him down in an indiscriminate hail of fire. Even if she survived a bullet wound, it would cripple her for life. She'd rather die.

The moment had almost arrived, bringing with it a sharp taste of anticipation.

Her stage fright always evaporated once the curtain was up.

But this waiting was a torment. Men, at least, could smoke through their tension. Opening her handbag, she took out a small bottle of perfume and touched the stopper behind her ears. Its cool, glassy edge felt like her only point of contact with tangible reality. An instant later she caught the scent of Cape Jasmine.

She took off her coat and dabbed some more perfume in the crooks of her elbows. Before she'd had time to put it back on, she saw, through the tiers of a white display-model wedding cake in the window, a car parked outside the café. It was his.

She gathered up her coat and handbag, and walked out with them over her arm. By the time she approached, the driver had opened the door for her. Mr. Yee was sitting in the middle of the backseat.

"I'm late, I know," he muttered, stooping slightly in apology.

She sent him a long, accusing look, then got in. After the driver had returned to his seat, Mr. Yee told him to drive to Ferguson Road—presumably to the apartment where their last assignation had taken place.

"I need to get to a jeweler's first," she told him in a low voice. "I want to replace a diamond stud that's fallen out of one of my earrings. There's a place just here. I would have gone before you got here, but I was afraid I might miss you. So I ended up waiting for ages on my own, like an idiot."

He laughed. "I'm sorry—just as I was leaving, a couple of people I needed to see showed up." He leaned forward to speak to the chauffeur: "Go back to where we just came from." They had already driven some distance away.

"Everything's always so difficult," she pouted. "We're never private at home, there's never a chance to say a word to each other. I want to go back to Hong Kong. Can you get me a boat ticket?"

"Missing the husband?"

"Don't talk to me about him!"

She had told Mr. Yee she was taking revenge for her husband's indiscretion with a dancing girl.

As they sat next to each other in the back of the car, he folded his arms so that his elbow nudged against the fullest part of her breast. This was a familiar trick of his: to sit primly upright while covertly enjoying the pleasurable softness of her.

She twisted around to look out the window, to tell the chauffeur exactly where to stop. The car made a U-turn at the next crossroads, and then another a little farther on to get them back to the P'ing-an, the only respectable second-run cinema in the city. The building's dull red facade curved inward, like a sickle blade set upon the street corner. Opposite was Commander K'ai's Café again, with the Siberian Leather Goods Store and the Green House Ladies' Clothing Emporium next, each fronted by two large display windows filled with glamorously dressed mannequins bent into all manner of poses beneath neon signs. The next-door establishment was smaller and far more nondescript. Although the sign over the door said JEWELER'S, its single display window was practically empty.

He told the chauffeur to stop the car, then got out and followed her inside. Though, in her high-heeled shoes, she was half a head taller than him, he clearly did not mind the disparity in their heights. Tall men, she had found in her experience, liked girls who were small, while short men seemed to prefer their women to tower over them—perhaps out of a desire for balance. She knew he was watching her, and so slightly exaggerated the swivel of her hips as she sashayed through the glass doors like a sea dragon.

An Indian dressed in a Western-style suit greeted them. Though the shop was small, its interior was light, high-ceilinged, and almost entirely bare. It was fitted out with just one waist-high glass showcase, toward the back, in which were displayed some birthstones, one for each month of the year—semiprecious yellow quartz, or red or blue gems made of sapphire or ruby dust, supposed to bring good luck.

She took out of her bag a pear-shaped ruby earring, at the top of which a diamond-studded leaf was missing one stone.

"We can get one to match it," the Indian said, after taking a look.

When she asked how much it would cost and when it would be ready, Mr. Yee added: "Ask him if he has any decent rings." As he had chosen to study in Japan, rather than Britain or the United

States, he felt uncomfortable speaking English and always got other people to interpret for him.

She hesitated. "Why?"

He smiled. "I said I wanted to buy you a ring, didn't I? A diamond ring—a decent one."

After another pause, she gave an almost stoic, resigned smile, then softly asked: "Do you have any diamond rings?"

The Indian shouted a startling, incomprehensible stream of what sounded like Hindi upstairs, then escorted them up.

To one side of the cream-colored back wall of the showroom was a door leading to a pitch-dark staircase. The office was on a little mezzanine set between the two floors of the building, with a shallow balcony overlooking the shop floor—presumably for surveillance purposes. The wall immediately to their left as they entered was hung with two mirrors of different sizes, each painted with multicolored birds and flowers and inscribed with gilded Chinese calligraphy: THIS ROC WILL SURELY SOAR TEN THOUSAND MILES. CONGRATULATIONS, MR. BADA, ON YOUR GRAND OPENING. RESPECTFULLY, CH'EN MAO-K'UN. Too tall for the room's sloping ceiling, a third large mirror, decorated with a phoenix and peonies, had been propped up against another wall.

To the front of the room, a desk had been placed along the ebony railing, with a telephone and a reading lamp resting on top. Next to it was a tea table on which sat a typewriter, covered with an old piece of glazed cloth. A second, squat Indian, with a broad ashen-brown face and a nose squashed like a lion's muzzle, stood up from his round-backed armchair to move chairs over for them.

"So it is diamond rings you are interested in. Sit down, please, sit down." He waddled slowly off to a corner of the room, his stomach visibly preceding him, then bent over a low green ancient-looking safe.

This, clearly, was not a high-class establishment. Though Mr. Yee appeared unfazed by his dingy surroundings, Chia-chih felt a twinge of embarrassment that she had brought him here. These days, she'd heard, some shops were just a front for black marketers or speculators.

Wu had selected this store for its proximity to Commander K'ai's Café. As she'd walked up the stairs, it had occurred to her that on his way back down they would catch him as easily as a turtle in a jar. As he would probably insist on walking in front of her, he would step first into the show-room. There, a couple of male customers brows-ing the display cabinet would suddenly move out to block his way. But two men couldn't spend too long pretending to choose cheap cuff links, tie pins, and trinkets for absent lady-friends; they couldn't dawdle indecisively like girls. Their entrance needed to be perfectly timed: neither too late nor too early. And once they were in, they had to stay in. Patrolling up and down outside was not an option; his chauffeur would quickly get suspicious. Their best delaying tactic was probably gazing at the window display of the leather shop next door, several yards behind the car.

Sitting to one side of the desk, she couldn't help turning to look down over the balcony. Only the shop window fell within her line of vision. As the window was clear and its glass shelves empty, she could see straight out to the pavement, and to the edge of the car parked next to it.

Then again, perhaps two men shopping alone would look far too conspicuous. They might draw the attention not only of the chauffeur, but also of Mr. Yee himself, from the balcony upstairs, who might then grow suspicious and delay his return downstairs. A stalemate would be catastrophic. Perhaps they would catch him instead at the entrance to the shop. In which case their timing would need to be even more perfect. They would need to approach at a walk, as the sound of running footsteps would instantly alert the chauffeur. Mr. Yee had brought only his driver with him, so perhaps the latter was doubling as a bodyguard.

Or maybe the two of them would split up, one of them lingering in front of the Green House Ladies' Clothing Emporium arm in arm with Lai

Hsiu-chin, her eyes glued to the window display. A girl could stand for minutes on end staring at clothes she couldn't afford, while her boyfriend waited impatiently, his back to the shop window, looking around him.

All these scenarios danced vaguely through her mind, even as she realized that none of this was her concern. She could not lose the feeling that, upstairs in this little shop, she was sitting on top of a powder keg that was about to blow her sky-high. A slight tremble was beginning to take hold of her legs.

The shop assistant had gone back downstairs. The boss was much darker skinned than his assistant; they did not look to be father and son. The younger man had saggy, stubbled, pouchlike cheeks and heavy-lidded, sleepy-looking eyes. Though not tall, he was built sturdily enough to serve, if necessity arose, as security guard. The position of the jewelry cabinet so near the back of the shop and the bare window display suggested that they were afraid of being robbed, even in daylight; a padlock hung by the door, for use at night. So there must be something of value on the premises: probably gold bars, U.S. dollars, and silver.

She watched as the Indian brought out a black velvet tray, around a foot long, inlaid with rows of diamond rings. She and Mr. Yee leaned in.

Seeing their lack of interest—neither picked one up to have a closer look—the proprietor put the tray back in the safe. "I've this one, too," he added, opening a small blue velvet box. Set deep within was a pink diamond, the size of a pea.

No one was selling pink diamonds at the moment, she remembered Yee Tai-tai saying. After her initial astonishment had passed, she felt a rush of relief—that the shop had, in the end, come through for her. Until the pink diamond, she had looked like an incompetent bounty hunter, a Cantonese nobody dragging her powerful Shanghai sugar daddy to a tatty gemstone boutique. Of course, the moment the gun sounded, everything—including all peripheral thoughts of plausibility, of pride—would shatter. Although she understood this well enough, she could not allow herself to think about it, for fear that he would see the terror on her face.

She picked up the ring. He laughed softly as he looked at the stone in her hand: "Now that's more like it." She felt a numb chill creeping up the back of her head; the display windows downstairs and the glass door between them seemed to be broadening out, growing taller, as if behind her were an enormous, two-story-high expanse of brilliant, fragile glass, ready to disintegrate at any moment. But even as she felt almost dizzy with the precariousness of her situation, the shop seemed to be blanketing her in torpor. Inside she could hear only the muffled buzz of the city outside— because of the war, there were far fewer cars on the road than usual; the sounding of a horn was a rarity. The warm, sweet air inside the office pressed soporifically down on her like a quilt. Though she was vaguely aware that something was about to happen, her heavy head was telling her that it must all be a dream.

She examined the ring under the lamplight, turning it over in her fingers. Sitting by the balcony, she began to imagine that the bright windows and door visible behind her were a cinema screen across which an action movie was being shown. She had always hated violent films; as a child, she had turned her back whenever a scene became grisly.

"Six carats. Try it on," the Indian urged.

She decided to enjoy the drowsy intimacy of this jeweler's den. Her eyes flitted to the reflection of her foot, nestling amid clumps of peonies, in the mirror propped against the wall, then back to the fabulous treasure—worthy, surely, of a tale from the *Thousand and One Nights*—on her finger. She turned the ring this way, then that, comparing it to the rose red of her nail varnish. Though it seemed pale and small next to her brightly lacquered nails, inside the gloomy office it had an alluring sparkle, like a star burning pink in dusk light. She registered a twinge of regret that it was to be no more than a prop in the short, penultimate scene of the drama unfolding around it.

"So what do you think?" Mr. Yee said.

"What do you think?"

"I'm no expert. I'm happy if you like it."

"Six carats. I don't know whether there are any faults in it. I can't see any."

They leaned in together over the ring, talking and laughing like an engaged couple. Although she had been educated in Canton, the earliest treaty port to open to British traders, the schools there had not attached as much importance to teaching English as they did in Hong Kong, and she always spoke the language in timid, low tones. Sensing her lack of linguistic confidence, the proprietor decided to spare her his usual negotiating preamble on the whys-and-wherefores of diamond-costing. A price was quickly agreed upon: eleven gold bars, to be delivered tomorrow. If any individual bars turned out to fall below the regulation weight, Mr. Yee pledged to make up the difference; likewise, the jeweler promised to reimburse them for any that were too heavy. The entire transaction—trading gold for diamonds—felt like another detail stolen from the *Arabian Nights*.

She worried that the whole thing had been wrapped up too quickly. They probably weren't expecting her and Yee to reemerge so soon. Dialogue, she knew, was the best filler of stage time.

"Shall we ask for a receipt?" He would probably be thinking of sending someone over tomorrow, to deliver the gold and pick up the ring.

The Indian was already writing one out. The ring had also been taken off and returned to him.

They sat back next to each other in their chairs, relaxing in the postnegotiation détente.

She laughed softly. "These days no one wants anything but gold. They don't even want a cash deposit."

"Just as well. I never carry any on me."

She knew, from her experience of living with the Yees, that it was always the aides who covered incidental costs—it was a minister's privilege never to dig into his own pockets. Today, of course, he had come out alone, and therefore penniless, because of the need for secrecy.

The English say that power is an aphrodisiac. She didn't know whether this was true; she herself was entirely oblivious to its attractions. They also say that the way to a man's heart is through his stomach; that a man will fall easy prey to a woman who can cook. Somewhere in the first decade or two of the twentieth century, a well-known Chinese scholar was supposed to have added that the way to a woman's heart is through her vagina. Though his name escaped her, she could remember the analogy he had devised in defense of male polygamy: "A teapot is always surrounded by more than one cup."

She refused to believe that an intellectual would come out with something so vulgar. Nor did she believe the saying was true, except perhaps for desperate old prostitutes or merry widows. In her case, she had found Liang Jun-sheng repellent enough before the whole thing began, and afterward even more so.

Though maybe that was not a valid example, because Liang Jun-sheng had been anxious, insecure, painfully aware of her dislike from the outset. His obvious sense of inferiority only grew as things went along between them, increasing her contempt for him.

Surely she hadn't fallen in love with Yee? Despite her fierce skepticism toward the idea, she found herself unable to refute the notion entirely; since she had never been in love, she had no idea what it might feel like. Because, since her midteens, she had been fully occupied in repelling romantic offensives, she had built up a powerful resistance to forming emotional attachments. For a time, she had thought she might be falling for K'uang Yu-min, but she ended up hating him—for turning out just like the others.

The two occasions she had been with Yee, she had been so tense, so taken up in saying her lines that there had been no opportunity to ask herself how she actually felt. At the house, she had to be constantly on her guard. Every night she was expected to stay up socializing as late as everyone else. When she was finally released back to the privacy of her own room, she would gulp down a sleeping pill to guarantee herself a good night's sleep. Though K'uang Yu-min had given her a small bottle of them, he had told her to avoid taking them if she possibly could, in case anything were to happen in the morning for which a clear head would be required. But without them, she was tormented by insomnia, something she had never suffered from in the past.

Only now, as this last, tense moment of calm stretched infinitely out, on this cramped balcony, the artificial brightness of its lamplight contrasting grubbily with the pale sky visible through the door and windows downstairs, could she permit herself to relax and inquire into her own feelings. Somehow, the nearby presence of the Indian, bent over his writing desk, only intensified her sense of being entirely alone with her lover. But now was not the moment to ask herself whether she loved him; instead, she needed to—

He was gazing off into the middle distance, a faintly sorrowful smile on his face. He had never dared dream such happiness would come his way in middle age. It was, of course, his power and position that he had principally to thank; they were an inseparable part of him. Presents, too, were essential, though they needed to be distributed at the correct moments. Given too soon, they carried within an insulting insinuation of greed. Though he knew perfectly well the rules of the game they were playing, he had to permit himself a brief moment of euphoria at the prize that had fallen into his lap; otherwise, the entire exercise was meaningless.

He was an old hand at this: taking his paramours shopping, ministering to their whims, retreating into the background while they made their choices. But there was, she noted again, no cynicism in his smile just then; only sadness. He sat in silhouette against the lamp, seemingly sunk into an attitude of tenderly affectionate contemplation, his downcast eyelashes tinged the dull cream of moths' wings as they rested on his gaunt cheeks.

He really loves me, she thought. Inside, she felt a raw tremor of shock—then a vague sense of loss.

It was too late.

The Indian passed the receipt to him. He placed it inside his jacket.

"Run," she said softly.

For a moment he stared, and then understood everything. Springing up, he barged the door open, steadied himself on the frame, then swung down to grab firm hold of the banister and stumbled down the dark, narrow stairs. She heard his footsteps break into a run, taking the stairs two or three at a time, thudding irregularly over the treads.

Too late. She had realized too late.

The jeweler was obviously bewildered. Conscious of how suspicious their behavior must look, she forced herself to sit still, resisting the temptation to look down.

They listened to the sound of shoes pounding on floor tiles until he burst into their line of vision, shooting out of the glass door like a cannonball. A moment later, the burly shop assistant also emerged into view, following close behind. She was terrified he might attempt to pull Yee back and ask him to explain himself; a delay of even a few seconds would be fatal. Intimidated, perhaps, by the sight of the official car, however, the Indian stopped in the store entrance, staring out, his heavy, muscular silhouette blocking the doorway. After that, all they heard was the screech of an engine, as if the vehicle were rearing up on its back wheels, followed by a bang. The slam of a door, perhaps—or a gunshot? Then the car roared off.

If it had been gunfire, they would have heard more than one shot.

She steadied herself. Quiet returned.

She heaved a sigh of relief; her entire body felt weak, exhausted, as if just recovered from serious illness. Carefully gathering up her coat and handbag, she smiled and nodded as she got up from her chair: "Tomorrow, then." She lowered her voice again, to its normal English-speaking mumble. "He'd forgotten about another appointment, so he needed to hurry."

The jeweler had already taken his eyeglass back out and adjusted the focus to ascertain that the gentleman just left had not first swapped the pink diamond ring for another. He then saw her smilingly out.

She couldn't blame him for wanting to make sure. The negotiations over price had been suspiciously brief and easy.

She hurried down the stairs. When the shop assistant saw her reappear he hesitated, then seemed to decide to say nothing. As she left, however, she heard shouting between upstairs and down.

There were no free pedicabs outside the shop, so she walked on toward Seymour Road. The group surely must have scattered the moment they saw him dash for the car and drive off; they would have realized that the game was up. She couldn't relax; what if someone had been assigned to watch the back door? What if they hadn't seen what had happened at the front, and hadn't yet left the scene? What would happen if she ran into him? But even if he suspected her of treachery, he wouldn't confront her there and then, much less summarily execute her.

She felt surprised that it was still light outside, as if inside the store she had lost all sense of time. The pavement around her was heaving with humanity; pedicab after pedicab rushed past on the road, all of them taken. Pedestrians and vehicles flowed on by, as if separated from her by a wall of glass, and no more accessible than the elegant mannequins in the window of the Green House

Ladies' Clothing Emporium—you could look, but you couldn't touch. They glided along, imperviously serene, as she stood on the outside, alone in her agitation.

She was on the watch for a charcoal-fired vehicle drawing suddenly up beside her, and for a hand darting out to pull her inside.

The pavement in front of the P'ing-an Theater was deserted: the audience was not yet spilling out at the end of a show, so no pedicabs were lined up outside, waiting for customers. Just as she was hesitating over which direction to walk in, she turned and saw that some distance away, along the opposite side of the street, an empty pedicab was slowly approaching, a red, blue, and white windmill tied to its handlebar. Seeing her wave and shout at him, the tall young cyclist hurried to cross over, the little windmill spinning faster as he accelerated toward her.

"Yu Garden Road," she told him as she got in.

Fortunately, while she'd been in Shanghai she'd had very little direct contact with the group, and so had never got around to mentioning that she had a relative living on Yu Garden Road. She thought she would stay there a few days, while she assessed the situation.

As the pedicab approached Ching-an Temple, she heard a whistle blow.

"The road's blocked," her cyclist told her.

A middle-aged man in a short mandarin jacket

was pulling a length of rope across the street, holding the whistle in his mouth. On the other side of the road, a second similarly dressed man pulled the other end of the rope straight to seal off the traffic and pedestrians within. Someone was lethargically ringing a bell, the thin, tinny sound barely carrying over the wide street.

Her pedicab driver cycled indomitably up to the rope, then braked and impatiently spun his windmill, before turning around to smile at her.

Three black capes were now sitting around the mahjong table. The nose of the new arrival — Liao Tai-tai — was speckled with white pockmarks.

"Mr. Yee's back," Ma Tai-tai smirked.

"What a wicked liar that Wang Chia-chih is!" Yee Tai-tai complained. "Promising to take us all out to dinner then running away. I'll collapse with hunger if she makes us wait much longer!"

"Mr. Yee." Liao Tai-tai smiled. "Your wife's bankrupted us all today. She'll be the one buying dinner tomorrow."

"Mr. Yee," Ma Tai-tai said, "where's the dinner you promised us last time you won? It's impossible to get a meal out of you."

"Mr. Yee ought to buy us dinner tonight, since we can never get him to accept our invitations," the other black cape said.

He merely smiled. After the maid brought him

43

tea, he knocked his cigarette ash onto the saucer, glancing across at the thick wool curtains covering the wall opposite and wondering how many assassins they could conceal. He was still shaken by the afternoon's events.

Tomorrow he must remember to have them taken down, though his wife was bound to object to something so expensive being sidelined into a storeroom.

It was all her fault, the result of her careless choice of friends. But even he was impressed by how elaborately, how far in advance—two years— the entire trap had been premeditated. The preparations had, indeed, been so perfectly thorough that only a last-minute change of heart on the part of his femme fatale had saved him. So she really had loved him—his first true love. What a stroke of luck.

He could have kept her on. He had heard or read somewhere that all spies are brothers; that spies can feel a loyalty to one another stronger than the causes that divide them. In any case, she was only a student. Of that group of theirs, only one had been in the pay of Chungking, the one who had gotten away—the single glitch in the entire operation. Most likely he'd stepped out of the P'ing-an halfway through a showing, then gone back into the theater once the assassination attempt was aborted. After the area was sealed off, he would have shown the police his ticket stub and then been allowed to slip away. The young man who'd waited with him to do the job had seen him check that the stub was safely stashed along with his cigarettes. It had been agreed in advance that he wouldn't take up room in the getaway car; that afterward he would stroll inconspicuously back into the cinema. After they'd been roughed up a bit, the little idiots came out with the whole story.

Mr. Yee stood behind his wife, watching the game. After he had stubbed out his cigarette, he took a sip of his tea; still too hot. Though an early night was surely what he needed, he was over-tired, unable to wind down. He was exhausted from sitting by the phone all afternoon waiting for news; he hadn't even had a proper dinner. As soon as he'd reached safety, he'd immediately tele-phoned to get the whole area sealed off. By ten o'clock that evening they'd all been shot. She must have hated him at the end. But real men have to be ruthless. She wouldn't have loved him if he'd been the sentimental type.

And, of course, his hands had been tied — more by Chou Fo-hai than by the Japanese military police. For some time Chou had been directing his own secret-service operation, and saw Gov-ernment Intelligence — Mr. Yee's department — as an irrelevance. Consequently, he kept an oppres-sively close eye on them, always on the lookout for evidence of incompetence. Mr. Yee could imagine all too easily what use Chou would have made of the discovery that the head of Domestic Intelligence had given house-room to an assassin's plant.

Now, at least, Chou could find no grounds on which to reproach him. If he accused him of executing potentially useful witnesses, he could confidently counter that they'd been only students; they weren't experienced spies from whom a slow, reasoned torture could have spilled useful information. And if the executions had been delayed, word of the affair might have gotten out. They would have become patriotic heroes plotting to assassinate a national traitor; a rallying point for popular discontent.

He was not optimistic about the way the war was going, and he had no idea how it would turn out for him. But now that he had enjoyed the love of a beautiful woman, he could die happy—without regret. He could feel her shadow forever near him, comforting him. Even though she had hated him at the end, she had at least felt something. And now he possessed her utterly, primitively— as a hunter does his quarry, a tiger his kill. Alive, her body belonged to him; dead, she was his ghost.

"Take us out to dinner, Mr. Yee! Take us out!" the three black capes chirruped ferociously. "He promised last time!"

"So did Ma Tai-tai," Yee Tai-tai smilingly intervened, "then when we didn't see her for a few days, we forgot all about it."

"Ever the loyal wife." Ma Tai-tai smiled back.

"Look, is Mr. Yee going to take us to dinner or not?"

"Mr. Yee has certainly had a run of luck lately," Ma Tai-tai pronounced, looking at him and smiling again. They understood each other perfectly. She could hardly have failed to notice the two of them disappearing, one after the other. And the girl still wasn't back. He had looked distracted when he returned, the elation still glimmering over his face. This afternoon, she guessed, had been their first assignation.

He reminded himself to drill his wife on the official story he had made up: that Mai Tai-tai had needed to hurry back to Hong Kong to take care of urgent family business. Then, to frighten her a bit with some secret-service patter: that not long after she invited this viper into the bosom of their home, he had received intelligence that she was part of a Chungking spy ring. Just as his people had begun to make further inquiries, he had heard that the Japanese had gotten wind of it. If he hadn't struck first, he would have gotten none of the credit for the intelligence work already done, and the Japanese might have discovered the connection with his wife, and tried to incriminate him. Best lay it on thick, so that she didn't listen to Ma Tai-tai's gossip.

"Take us to dinner, Mr. Yee! Stop getting your wife to do your dirty work."

"My wife gives her own dinners. She's promised you tomorrow."

"We know how busy you are, Mr. Yee. You tell us when you're free, and we'll be there; any day after tomorrow."

"No, take us tonight. How about Lai-hsi?"

"The only edible thing there is the cold buffet."

"German food is boring—nothing but cold cuts. How about somewhere Hunanese, just for a change?"

"Or there's Shu-yü—Ma Tai-tai didn't come with us yesterday."

"I'd rather Chiu-ju—I haven't been there for ages."

"Didn't Yang Tai-tai hold a dinner at Chiu-ju?"

"Last time we went, we didn't have Liao Tai-tai with us. We needed someone from Hunan—we didn't know what to order."

"It's too spicy for me!"

"Then tell the chef to make it less spicy."

"Only cold fish won't eat hot chili!"

Amid the raucous laughter, he quietly slipped out.

LUST, CAUTION

A Screenplay by Wang Hui Ling and James Schamus

Based on a Short Story by Eileen Chang

Ext. Yee's Residence—Shanghai—Winter 1942—Day

A German Shepherd guard dog, straining at his leash, sniffs the ground.

Yu Yuen Road. Lane #1136. A cluster of elegant residences sits under gray skies. Once the height of Shanghai fashion and wealth, but now slightly seedy.

In front of every house there stands a security guard with a gun. And on the rooftops, guards with binoculars, keeping watch.

Plainclothes security, in their short coats, idle, cold and surly. An air of menace.

By the high wall, two chauffeurs smoke and chat idly, leaning on their fancy cars.

Int. Yee's Residence—Shanghai—Day

Wontons float in bowls of chicken soup. Amah, the house-keeper, picks up the bowls and heads down the corridor. Laughter mixes with the noise of mahjong tiles clacking— a game in progress.

Ma Tai-tai (O.S.—offscreen)

Aiya! And I was waiting to nab your "2"!

(A "Tai-tai" is a married woman with a certain social status—"Ma Tai-tai" means something like "Madame Ma.")

YEE TAI-TAI (O.S.)

Shameless! Like I didn't know you were missing a "2"?
If only Mai Tai-tai didn't block me . . .

LEUNG TAI-TAI (O.S.)

Aiya! Don't you know three "pung" can't beat one good
"stash"! So much for that! Come, come! Let's shift the
wind and change seats!

Amah enters the chamber, lit by a pool of light over the mahjong table.

Amah sets down the tray while signaling for another servant
to remove leftover bowls of red dates and sticky rice. The
white porcelain spoons and bowls are all stained with red
lipstick.

On the mahjong table, the ladies' smooth white hands are
busily shuffling and sorting the tiles, their diamond rings
sparkling under the sharp light.

MA TAI-TAI (O.S.)

Talking about wind shift, I almost forgot to congratu-
late you!—on Mr. Leung's promotion!

LEUNG TAI-TAI

What promotion, really!

(snickers)

An officer in charge of rice!

MA TAI-TAI

Look, these days we can't even get Indian rice through our connections! Controlling rice is more powerful than guarding gold!

Just you listen to our Yee Tai-tai.

YEE TAI-TAI

(laughs)

Listen to me? Why, I'm no living Buddha! If anyone, your husband should have listened to me, and not taken on Transportation. Now he's away from home two, three days a week—and lets you run wild!

We now get a look at the ladies. Yee Tai-tai, the hostess, is a grand dame, older than the others, and jealous of her superior status. Leung Tai-tai is corpulent, avaricious, and grasping. Ma Tai-tai is younger, attractive, and sharp-eyed.

MA TAI-TAI

Me, wild? His relatives come over every day for one thing or another, till my hallways are crammed with in-laws. Finding odd jobs for them is not enough, I have to feed them too. We don't earn enough for all that bother.

LEUNG TAI-TAI

You said it!

YEE TAI-TAI

Aiya! We can't give our Mai Tai-tai the wrong impression—she'll think Wang Ching-wei's government is run by us wives over the mahjong table!

WANG CHIA-CHIH/MAI TAI-TAI

But it seems you're only telling the truth!

LEUNG TAI-TAI

Those little Japanese devils will never know—that there's another heaven above the Emperor's head!

The women crack up.

We now see to whom Yee Tai-tai is referring. Mai Tai-tai is only in her early twenties, delicately beautiful, and wearing hardly any makeup besides the bright shiny lipstick on her chiseled lips. She smiles demurely at Yee Tai-tai, something slightly secretive in her manner—in fact, more than slightly, as we shall discover. For her real name is Wang Chia-chih, and the money she is gambling on mahjong today is not her own. . . .

YEE TAI-TAI

Eat it while it's still hot.

LEUNG TAI-TAI

I really shouldn't eat any more! So fat already—

YEE TAI-TAI

Everybody is hoarding these days! Since we can't do much else, we might as well hoard fat on our bodies!

WANG CHIA-CHIH/MAI TAI-TAI

What's good to hoard these days, Yee Tai-tai? My Little Mai is always looking for the next trend in imports. Even with the port closed, you can still do a lot of business in Hong Kong.

YEE TAI-TAI

You said you already sold out all your Western medicine? What a shortage! I'd just have him get more of that for you.

From the corner of her eyes Ma Tai-tai watches the two confer.

MA TAI-TAI

I heard you all went to that Szechuan restaurant Shu-yü yesterday?

YEE TAI-TAI

Yes, we did, the whole group—Mai Tai-tai had never been there before.

WANG CHIA-CHIH/MAI TAI-TAI

When I told them, they all laughed—

YEE TAI-TAI

They've already opened two branches in Hong Kong—

WANG CHIA-CHIH/MAI TAI-TAI

I know—

YEE TAI-TAI

They said the Szechuan chefs couldn't get along with
the Hong Kong chefs, so business was bad. Hong Kong
people can't take it too spicy hot anyway, right? It was
plenty hot yesterday—

WANG CHIA-CHIH/MAI TAI-TAI

Very hot indeed!—So hot that I—

YEE TAI-TAI

The colder it gets, the hotter one eats—to take the
chill out! Their spicy bean fish was so good! Why, who
just discarded the "5 dots"? Aiyo! Thank you very
much!

She puts down her bowl to rearrange the tiles.

Ma and Leung both sport fashionable black capes, closed at the
collar with a thick gold clasp.

LEUNG TAI-TAI

So Ma Tai-tai didn't go yesterday?

YEE TAI-TAI

She's been hiding from us for quite a while!

MA TAI-TAI

I was tied up at home!

YEE TAI-TAI

(laughs)

You promised to treat us, couldn't back down, so instead you vanished!

MA TAI-TAI

And who was busy when I called a few days ago?

YEE TAI-TAI

(laughs)

That didn't count—I had to fetch Mai Tai-tai. Ask her if you don't believe me.

(to Mai Tai-tai/Wang Chia-chih)

Ma Tai-tai picked that very day to treat us, deliberately!

LEUNG TAI-TAI

(to Mai)

Say, any stockings left from your stock?

WANG CHIA-CHIH/MAI TAI-TAI

I'm afraid I'm all sold out of those too.

Yee Tai-tai

Yesterday Liao Tai-tai alone took away half a dozen!

Leung Tai-tai

That lady is just too . . .

Wang Chia-chih/Mai Tai-tai

(apologetic)

I'll bring more next time, I promise!

Yee Tai-tai

Shanghai is short of just about everything these days. Even toothpaste—you can only get it on the black market. Now that I found you again, you must come more often, and always stay with me when you're in town!

Ma lowers her eyelids and fiddles with the tiles in her hand.

Mai Tai-tai (Wang Chia-chih) follows Ma's every expression. Clearly, Ma makes her nervous.

Sound cut: on the clattering of mahjong tiles, we cut to:

Int. Basement Hallway—Secret Service Building—Shanghai—Day

An iron door is pushed open and a man exits into a hallway— Yee, forties, elegant, pale, and weary. He winces almost imperceptibly at the sounds of torture emanating from the room behind him. He is accompanied by his second-in-command, Chang, sinister, oily.

This is a basement prison operated by the Wang Ching-wei regime's secret service.

CHANG

He won't last much longer—the Japanese military will be here to claim him.

YEE

They didn't say dead or alive. Give him a quick one as a favor.

Chang glances at Yee.

CHANG

Sir, about General Miura Taicho—they are still looking for the American shipment of arms to Chungking.

YEE

I'll see him tonight.

CHANG

His secretary called. He regrets that he will have to cancel tonight's dinner. He asks that you report first thing tomorrow morning—at Japanese headquarters.

Yee pauses, vaguely disturbed.

INT./EXT. SECRET SERVICE BUILDING—FRONT COURTYARD— SHANGHAI—DAY

Yee and Chang come down the stairs into the office area.

CHANG

Will you be returning today?

YEE

No. . . . I have an appointment.

As Yee heads toward his car, two bodyguards come quickly forward, checking the surroundings and opening the car door for him. Chang stands beside the car as Yee gets in.

The door closes, a bodyguard gets in the front with the driver.

Chang watches as Yee's car pulls away.

INT. YEE'S CAR—DAY

Yee sits in the backseat, searches his pockets, doesn't find what he is looking for.

The guard hands him a cigarette.

Yee lights it and smokes, thinking. He watches the pigeons circling above.

EXT. YEE'S RESIDENCE—SHANGHAI

Yee's car pulls up at the entrance. Another car is already parked in the alley.

The bodyguard gets out first, looks around, then opens the car door.

Yee gets out, alert, and disappears into the house in a single stride.

INT. YEE'S RESIDENCE—SHANGHAI—CONTINUOUS

Yee pauses in the front hall, hears the women laughing and playing.

In the hallway mirror, he straightens his hair.

He walks upstairs. Amah is passing by.

> AMAH

Sir, you're back home.

> LEUNG TAI-TAI (O.S.)

Someone helped my cousin buy a yellow diamond from a Russian aristocrat, some seven or eight carats.

> MA TAI-TAI

Those Russian aristocrats are all over the place, scrounging for cigarette butts. Are you sure it wasn't a fake?

Yee enters, nods at the three ladies.

> YEE

I see you ladies started early today.

Mai Tai-tai (Wang Chia-chih) nods politely at him, and immediately lowers her eyes to sort the tiles in her hands.

Yee smiles, and stands behind Yee Tai-tai watching the game.
Yee Tai-tai discards a "3 character."

LEUNG TAI-TAI

Oh my god! You must have a great hand. Mr. Yee is here
to cheer you on.

MAI TAI-TAI/WANG CHIA-CHIH

Oh—my turn?

She quickly discards a tile.
Yee Tai-tai continues to talk diamonds.

YEE TAI-TAI

(looking at Ma's hand)

Now yours is something else! How many carats is it
again? Three?

Ma smiles uneasily, giving Yee a sly glance.

MA TAI-TAI

This old thing? It's so old-fashioned. I'm planning on
having it reset in a few days.

YEE TAI-TAI

Our trusted runner P'in Fen was here the other day
and showed me a five-carat. It was big all right, but the
brilliance was nowhere near yours—

Yee Tai-tai takes another look at Ma's diamond ring.

LEUNG TAI-TAI

And why didn't you call me?

YEE TAI-TAI

I only had time for a quick look myself—"Pung"!

MA TAI-TAI

They all say P'in Fen brings in better goods than the shops! Mine is quite ordinary.

YEE TAI-TAI

As a runner she brings them to our door, saves us the hassle, and lets us check them out for a couple of days. P'in Fen has things that others don't. But the "hot oil" diamond last time? He wouldn't buy it.

Yee Tai-tai raises her eyes to her husband with a quick look of disdain.

The mahjong table appears to have become a diamond exhibition. Only Mai Tai-tai has no diamond on her finger, just a jade ring.

YEE TAI-TAI

You have any idea how much these go for now? A flawless yellow diamond can go up to over ten taels, ten taels of gold a carat. P'in Fen claims that yellow and pink diamonds are in hot demand but there's no

63

supply. You just can't find any. Those who have them hoard them rather than sell!

YEE

(smiles)

That "hot oil" of yours must have weighed over ten carats. A diamond is not a quail egg, it's a stone after all. If you wore that on your finger you could hardly play mahjong.

YEE TAI-TAI

Right! You wouldn't buy it and you still give me an earful!

Yee Tai-tai discards a "5 dots" and Leung Tai-tai quickly flips over all her tiles with a crash to declare victory.

LEUNG TAI-TAI

I win! . . .

MA TAI-TAI

Aiya! What a slip—all your fault, Mr. Yee, for saying diamonds are bad for mahjong!

Laughing and bitching, the ladies count their chips.

YEE TAI-TAI

He's here to spoil our game!

LEUNG TAI-TAI

Thank you, Mr. Yee!

MA TAI-TAI

That's not nice! Mr. Yee better treat us to dinner!

YEE

No problem. Just tell me where you would like to go.

LEUNG TAI-TAI

Shu-yü.

MA TAI-TAI

Not Shu-yü, someplace more expensive.

Yee suddenly darts his eyes toward the door.

Mai Tai-tai (Wang Chia-chih) turns her eyes from Yee back to her chips as she counts them, keeping one eye on the two black capes. She sips her tea, pauses, then glances at the clock on the wall.

MAI TAI-TAI/WANG CHIA-CHIH

Oh dear! How did it skip my mind? I have a meeting at three and forgot clean about it!

YEE TAI-TAI

(raising her voice)

Impossible. Why didn't you say so before? This is simply not done!

MAI TAI-TAI/WANG CHIA-CHIH

It's an important meeting—I totally forgot. I'm so
sorry. Mr. Yee, please take my place for a few hands—
I'll be back as soon as possible.

LEUNG TAI-TAI

(whining)

And I thought my luck was back!

MAI TAI-TAI/WANG CHIA-CHIH

It's Little Mai's money. After all these years, finally
we're getting part of it back.

YEE TAI-TAI

Well, not unless Liao Tai-tai can come.

(calls for Amah in Shanghainese)

Amah, please call Liao Tai-tai!

(to Mai Tai-tai)

When she arrives you may leave.

Ma turns around to light a cigarette, toying with the chips in
her hand. Ma's eyes meet Wang's for a brief moment.

MAI TAI-TAI/WANG CHIA-CHIH

Mr. Yee will stand in for me. It's so late already—I'm
afraid they won't wait!

Mai Tai-tai (Wang Chia-chih) checks the clock.

YEE

I'm afraid I can't be of help today. I have another engagement. I'll play all night with you ladies some other time.

YEE TAI-TAI

(to Wang Chia-Chih/Mai Tai-tai)

You're so bad! All right, all right, just go. But you have to buy us dinner.

LEUNG TAI-TAI

Yeah, I agree.

MA TAI-TAI

Aiya! Yee Tai-tai is really upset! No more special allowances, not even for her!

MAI TAI-TAI/WANG CHIA-CHIH

Sure, sure! I promise, dinner is on me tonight. Mr. Yee, please take my place, or else you won't be invited tonight!

Mai Tai-Tai (Wang Chia-chih) seizes the moment, gets up, apologizes, and quickly leaves.

LEUNG TAI-TAI

Do help, Mr. Yee! Stay awhile—see, Yee Tai-tai is already phoning around for a replacement.

YEE

I really am tied up. I came back just to change for an appointment.

MA TAI-TAI

I had a feeling Mr. Yee would be too occupied.

Wang overhears this last remark as she leaves the living room.

INT. YEE'S RESIDENCE—GUEST ROOM—SHANGHAI—1942—DAY

Wang quickly goes upstairs to the guest room.

She throws a few makeup items and perfume into her handbag.

She straps on her watch. She hears someone coming up the stairs, lowers her head, and keeps stuffing her bag with cigarettes and perfumes.

AMAH

(in Shanghainese)

Tai-tai says to let you use her car. It's waiting in front.

MAI TAI-TAI/WANG CHIA-CHIH

(mildly surprised, in Shanghainese)

Oh, that's very kind of her—but today Yee Tai-tai doesn't need to—very well then, thanks!

(not wishing to offend)

I'll be right down.

Wang checks herself in the mirror.

INT./EXT. YEE'S CAR—DAY

The car drives along a road flanked by bare plane trees.

> ### MAI TAI-TAI/WANG CHIA-CHIH
> #### *(in Shanghainese)*
>
> So few cars—in Hong Kong there's always so much traffic.

> ### CHAUFFEUR
> #### *(in Shanghainese)*
>
> No one can afford gas anymore.
>
> *(curious, looks into rear mirror)*
>
> Mai Tai-tai's Shanghainese is quite good.

> ### MAI TAI-TAI/WANG CHIA-CHIH
> #### *(smiling)*
>
> My mother's from Shanghai. My family moved to Hong Kong when the Japanese came.

> ### CHAUFFEUR
>
> I see.

Ext. Concessions Guard Station—Shanghai—Continuous

Traffic slows as they approach the French Concession. Wang waits in the car at a checkpoint manned by Japanese soldiers.

Cars with Japanese flags are waved past. The others wait in line.

Wang sees a bayonet pointing at a kneeling man whose luggage is being searched. At his side there is a dead body, lying in a pool of blood.

Int./Ext. Yee's Car—Continuous

The car enters the French Concession.

Long lines of people queue on the street, many of them foreigners wearing arm bands, waiting for bread, bracing themselves against the autumn chill. Wang Chia-chih ponders them.

Chauffeur

(in Shanghainese)

Look! For their love of bread these foreigners have to stand in line! They are only allowed to withdraw twenty yuans a day from the bank. They can no longer afford ham, so they settle for dry hard bread!

Int./Ext. Yee's Car—Keissling Café—Shanghai—Day

The car pulls over in front of the café. Wang gets out.

CHAUFFEUR

(in Shanghainese)

Shall I come back for you later?

MAI TAI-TAI/WANG CHIA-CHIH

No, you don't have to bother. I'll get a cab, no problem—thanks again!

Wang watches the car leave. She walks over to the café on the other side of the street. Cautiously she takes in her surroundings.

INT. KEISSLING CAFÉ—SHANGHAI—DAY

Wang pushes open the door and enters the posh Russian café.

A waiter approaches and motions her to an empty table.

WAITER

(in English)

Please.

She removes her hat and coat, looks out the window and checks that the car is gone, then turns and sits down at a table.

The café is practically empty, except for an elderly Western couple. Tango music plays on the radio. A waiter saunters over.

MAI TAI-TAI/WANG CHIA-CHIH

(in English)

Coffee please.

WAITER

Sure.

She looks out the window. Coffee is served. She looks at her watch—it's almost four.

WANG CHIA-CHIH

May I borrow your phone?

WAITER

Of course.

The waiter points at the counter. She looks up and sees the phone on the bar counter. Two Russian chefs on break are drinking liquor and chatting in Russian. She hesitates for a moment, then walks over to the phone.

She picks up the phone and dials.

A waiter behind the bar is drying glasses. After four rings, Wang hangs up. She mutters to herself before dialing again.

WANG CHIA-CHIH

That's odd—did I dial the wrong number?

Wang dials again. It rings, a click is heard, and someone answers.

K'UANG YU-MIN (O.S.)

Hello?

Wang speaks in Cantonese.

WANG CHIA-CHIH

Hi! Second Brother! It's me!

Wang deliberately turns her back to the two Russian chefs who have been eyeing her with interest.

WANG CHIA-CHIH

I'm calling from Keissling Café. Everything okay at home?

Two new customers walk in the door. Wang stiffens a bit.

WANG CHIA-CHIH

I'm fine!—Just too busy to call!

Wang eyes the couple, now seated.

WANG CHIA-CHIH

I plan to pick up that package today. Yes, it's all set—for now!

Wang stops for a moment and glances at the bare trees outside. The air is cold and damp. Passersby walk on briskly.

WANG CHIA-CHIH

(pause)

Yes . . .

A moment of silence.

WANG CHIA-CHIH

Anything—else?

Intercut:

We finally see who she's talking to:

INT. SUNRISE BOOKSTORE—UPSTAIRS ROOM— SHANGHAI—SAME

We're in the stockroom upstairs of a crammed bookstore—piles of books everywhere. A handsome young man, K'uang Yu-min, speaks into the phone.

K'UANG YU-MIN

. . . No . . . nothing.

INT. KEISSLING CAFÉ—SHANGHAI—CONTINUOUS

WANG CHIA-CHIH

. . . I guess I'd better leave now. . . . All right. See you later!

Wang Chia-chih holds the phone in her hand, then gently hangs up and walks back to her table. She sits, and stirs her coffee.

INT. SUNRISE BOOKSTORE—UPSTAIRS—CONTINUOUS

K'uang Yu-min hangs up the phone and is silent for a moment.
Wide:

A group of men, some standing, some sitting on makeshift seats, waits for him to say something. A young woman stands among them.

He nods.

> K'UANG YU-MIN

It's now.

The men rise. A couple of them check their guns in their holsters. Two others take small axes, hide them in their long sleeves. There are others in the room, watching the preparations nervously, whom we will recognize later on, including the young woman, Lai Hsiu-chin, and some other young men, Ou-yang, Liang, Huang Lei.

INT. KEISSLING CAFÉ—SHANGHAI—LATER

Wang sits at the table, takes a bottle of perfume from her purse, dips in a glass rod, and puts a few drops behind her ears.

She dips once more and puts some on her wrists.

Wang looks out of the window. We hold on her face, quietly searching the crowded street.

Fade out.

TITLE: Four Years Earlier

EXT. NARROW ROAD IN COUNTRYSIDE—OCTOBER 1938—DAY

A convoy of trucks, packed with students from Lingnan University fleeing for Hong Kong ahead of the oncoming

Japanese troops, pulls over to let pass a military column of young men in uniform heading for the front.

The students cheer them on, waving and shouting. The soldiers wave back.

Lai Hsiu-chin, a vivacious young student, suddenly jumps up, waving her handkerchief.

LAI HSIU-CHIN

(yelling)

Go beat those Japanese and when you come back we'll marry you!

Everybody tries to pull her back into the truck, while they giggle.

LAI HSIU-CHIN

I said we, not I, right? Well, the men all go off to war. Who'll be left to marry us?

The girls giggle, swaying and bumping against one another.

Wang Chia-chih sits among them, young, almost nondescript. She blushes but smiles along with the other girls.

EXT. ALONG THE ROAD BY A BROKEN BRIDGE—EVENING

At sunset all the trucks are backed up at a broken bridge. The students mill around waiting for the bridge to be fixed.

The teacher and truck driver study the map looking for alternative routes.

DRIVER

We can take this detour to Hong Kong.

TEACHER

The route doesn't matter, I just have to get these college kids there safely.

K'uang Yu-min, whom we saw at the bookstore earlier, runs and yells to the students.

K'UANG YU-MIN

Those who can help should come with me! Don't just stand there.

Rising smoke can be seen in the distance.

Later:

LAI HSIU-CHIN

The farmers' wives have cooked us sweet potatoes!

Lai and some female students are lugging over big pots of sweet potatoes donated by the peasants nearby.

Later:

The students huddle in small groups, refugees, sharing the food quietly.

Wang looks up at the darkening sky. The mountains slowly dissolve into shadows.

LAI HSIU-CHIN

Isn't your father in England? Why didn't he take you with him?

WANG CHIA-CHIH

He took my brother. After Mother died, he said he'd send for me. I waited for two years, and now, the war.

LAI HSIU-CHIN

I'll never go back home! This war gave me the chance to leave—and from Hong Kong, maybe I'll go and see the world.

EXT. HONG KONG UNIVERSITY—NOVEMBER 1938—DAY

To establish: panoramic view of the city of Hong Kong with Hong Kong University perched in the hills above.

EXT. HONG KONG UNIVERSITY CAMPUS—LATE AFTERNOON

Hong Kong students file out of the lecture rooms as Lingnan students wait to use their classrooms.

Wang and Lai walk together in the corridor.

LAI HSIU-CHIN

Meet you after class by the pond this evening?

WANG CHIA-CHIH

Okay.

K'uang Yu-min approaches.

K'UANG YU-MIN

Hi, Lai Hsiu-chin. I was hoping to run into you.

LAI HSIU-CHIN

K'uang Yu-min, you remember me?

K'UANG YU-MIN

Of course, I saw you onstage, with the women's theater group at Lingnan.

(hands Lai a flyer)

We just started a new drama club. Auditions tomorrow afternoon.

LAI HSIU-CHIN

But the women's group has never acted with men.

K'UANG YU-MIN

We're guest students here. There are so few of us already—we must work together.

LAI HSIU-CHIN

(excited)

Then let's do Ibsen's *A Doll's House*! I know Nora's lines inside out!

79

K'UANG YU-MIN

At times like this, who needs that kind of bourgeois drama! We want to put on a patriotic play, something to raise money for the resistance!

(notices Wang)

Why don't you come to the audition too?

WANG CHIA-CHIH

Oh, thank you, but I'm only a freshman. I haven't done much acting before.

K'UANG YU-MIN

Who cares! We must all pitch in. Our soldiers are fighting the enemy at the front, while these Hong Kongers continue with their lives of leisure.

(a sincere smile, a slight wave of his fist)

We have to wake them up with our drums and gongs!

K'uang walks away.

EXT. THE POND—HONG KONG UNIVERSITY—AUTUMN— NIGHT

Later, Wang and Lai chat by the pond.

LAI HSIU-CHIN

Typical of directors—never listens to anyone else. But since it's for the resistance, I suppose we women really shouldn't fall behind—but we'll probably just have to do what he says.

WANG CHIA-CHIH

He seems very passionate.

LAI HSIU-CHIN

His brother graduated from Whampoa Military Academy, but died fighting the Japanese. So his parents forbade him from enlisting in the army. That's why he's so worked up.

EXT. HONG KONG STREET—NIGHT

The girls walk down some steep steps toward the city. Lai Hsiu-chin sings as they walk.

LAI HSIU-CHIN

(singing)

The wind blows my hair.

WANG CHIA-CHIH

I better just concentrate on my studies.

LAI HSIU-CHIN

Come on! I know you want to be onstage just as much as me.

WANG CHIA-CHIH

But in Lingnan all I did was run lines for you upperclassmen. The instructor said I needed to work on my voice.

LAI HSIU-CHIN

Don't worry about it—just yell so the last row can hear you!

Lai Hsiu-chin and Wang Chia-chih both begin to sing again.

LAI HSIU-CHIN AND WANG CHIA-CHIH

(singing)

How can I not think about him?

INT. HONG KONG UNIVERSITY AUDITORIUM—EVENING

K'uang Yu-min and some other students in the theater group, including Liang Jun-sheng (pudgy, a bit sleazy-looking) and Ou-yang (a bit older, and already slightly balding) are rigging some lighting. They strain to lift the array, as Lai and some of the other girls stop to watch. Wang Chia-chih is reciting under her breath, trying to remember her lines.

WANG CHIA-CHIH

(mumbling to herself)

I give myself back to the land that nurtured me. In my soul . . .

K'uang directs the placement of the lights.

K'UANG YU-MIN

To the left, more to the left, more. . . . That's it!

Good, that's it, now try!

Suddenly, the theater goes dark, except for a dim spotlight on K'uang. Everyone quiets down—an unexpectedly magical moment.

Wang watches K'uang, enchanted.

The light dims.

INT. STUDENT HOSTEL ROOM—HONG KONG—DAY

The cramped room, filled with bunk beds.

Wang sits at her desk, books and papers spread out before her, a wrinkled letter in her hand, a photograph of a Chinese man with an English woman. She appears to have been crying, or at least holding back tears.

Lai rises from her bed.

LAI HSIU-CHIN

What is it?

Wang holds up the letter.

WANG CHIA-CHIH

My father got remarried. I'm writing him my congratulations.

Wang seals her aerogram and walks out alone.

INT. HONG KONG CINEMA—SUMMER—DAY

In the pitch-dark cinema, Wang sits alone, crying, watching the movie, an American melodrama.

EXT. OUTSIDE HONG KONG UNIVERSITY AUDITORIUM—SPRING—NIGHT

A large crowd of audience members file into the auditorium.

INT. BACKSTAGE AUDITORIUM—HONG KONG UNIVERSITY—EVENING

It's a madhouse.

Wang concentrates while she draws three lines across her brow.

K'uang does the same.

K'UANG YU-MIN

Once you put on the makeup, you are no longer yourself.

Liang Jun-sheng, while putting on Ou-yang's makeup, steals a glance over at Lai Hsiu-chin changing into her costume.

Wang, dressed in peasant clothes, wends her way to her starting position. The rest of the cast is ready and waiting.

Huang Lei hits the gong three times.

The curtain rises. A packed house. The Village Chief (Ou-yang) enters with the wounded K'uang Yu-min.

VILLAGE CHIEF

(knocks)

Mother Chao—

A village girl (Wang Chia-chih) quickly opens the door.

VILLAGE CHIEF

They found this officer on the mountains.

MOTHER CHAO/LAI HSIU-CHIN

Little Hong, is that your brother coming home?

WANG CHIA-CHIH

Shhh. Come on—hurry in.

The Village Chief brings the officer into the house.

VILLAGE CHIEF

Be careful.

MOTHER CHAO/LAI HSIU-CHIN

Oh my son! Hurry, go put on some hot water. How can you be wounded so badly?

VILLAGE CHIEF

He is an officer, not your son.

Later:

Evening light and shadow illuminate the stage. The Mother talks to herself on the doorsill, facing the audience.

MOTHER CHAO/LAI HSIU-CHIN

My son is coming home tonight, home for dinner! Let me kill a chicken to make him strong! My son is coming home, coming home tonight! My son is coming home, my son is going to come home.—Here, coo . . . coo— come here.

The Mother runs around the empty courtyard, clucking for a nonexistent chicken.

Wang Chia-chih has entered from the wings, accompanied by K'uang, dressed in an officer's uniform. After two days' rest, he is leaving. Wang takes her scarf and offers it to him.

WANG CHIA-CHIH

Since Mother learned of my brother's death, she's been sick.

K'uang nods and looks at her sympathetically.

In the wings Liang Jun-sheng places, with great care, the turntable needle onto an LP. He holds a microphone next to the turntable, and music wafts through the hall.

WANG CHIA-CHIH

I just finished knitting this for my brother, only—only he won't need it anymore.

(with tears)

Please take it with you!

K'UANG YU-MIN

I can't. You saved my life and I have nothing to give you in return.

WANG CHIA-CHIH

You've given everything to save China! Every time you kill an enemy, you are avenging my brother! I am only sorry that I am a girl. I need to take care of my mother, and I promised my brother he would never have to worry . . .

K'UANG YU-MIN

Your brother . . .

WANG CHIA-CHIH

He was the same age as you. Since Father died, he carried the whole family on his shoulders—he was such a fast worker that during harvest he was always the first to finish and had time to help the others. He was strong like you. . . . I followed him everywhere! He said heaven would always protect honest folks!

(sees tears welling in K'uang's eyes)

He was our only hope!

Suddenly Wang drops to her knees.

WANG CHIA-CHIH

Let me bow to you on behalf of our country, my dead brother, and our nation for generations and generations to come! China will not fall!

Choked with emotion, Wang's voice resonates around the hall. Audience members begin to stand and clap.

K'uang stoops to help her up. The two look at each other, holding hands.

AUDIENCE
(shouting)

China will not fall!

INT. NOODLE SHOP—HONG KONG—NIGHT

Outside, noodles are cooking over high flames. The friends drink up in real celebration.

THE GROUP

Bottoms up!

HUANG LEI

That was so great! A thousand people shouting "China will not fall!"

(raises his glass)

"China will not fall! China will not fall! China will not fall!"

K'uang Yu-min

Come on—only six hundred seats . . . plus some standing in the aisles. . . . Frankly, I underestimated those Hong Kong students.

Lai Hsiu-chin

The audience back in Lingnan was never this excited!

Wang Chia-chih

(earnestly)

Our story is our own story, which the audience can identify with. That's why they were so moved! I saw many of them still drying their eyes outside, making donations.

K'uang Yu-min

A toast to all of you! Finally we raised some donations. Now we can really do something!

Huang Lei

Let's drink it up tonight, and worry about the country tomorrow! Big Brother, Ganbei! Ganbei!

("Ganbei!" means "Cheers!")

Ou-yang

It's not just the resistance—it's our great acting that moved them. . . .

LIANG JUN-SHENG

We should sell tickets, and on the front of the door
have a big poster saying "Hot Ticket."

HUANG LEI

The tickets will be hot, not because of you, but because
of her.

(looking at Wang Chia-chi)

Give me the bottle! Come, let's toast to our leading lady!

THE GROUP

Our leading lady—cheers!

WANG CHIA-CHIH

No, no. I'm not! Cut it out!

Everyone laughs.

EXT. STREET IN HONG KONG—NIGHT

The friends, arm in arm, saunter down the street in the drizzly
night, singing patriotic songs.

THE GROUP

(singing)

There are clouds in the sky. Students in sweet youth
today, Pillars of society tomorrow. Tomorrow we'll
make waves to save our nation, Huge waves, huge

waves, forever surging! Fellow students, fellow
students—

Come forward with your strength now, And take into
our hands the fate of our land! Huge waves, huge waves,
forever surging!

A double-decker arrives and they scramble onboard.

THE GROUP

Hurry up! Hurry!

K'uang climbs straight onto the upper deck, with the others
following.

Ou-yang produces a cigarette ceremoniously from his pocket.
Huang Lei proffers a lighter. They crowd around to light the
cigarette.

LIANG JUN-SHENG

Is it lit? Ah!—

They take turns smoking the cigarette. Lai also takes a puff and
passes it to Wang. Wang hesitates, not knowing how to smoke.

LAI HSIU-CHIN

You can't be an artist and not smoke! Just try—it
comes in handy onstage.

Wang reluctantly takes a puff, and instantly coughs out the
smoke.

Lai holds the cigarette and runs back to the others.

LAI HSIU-CHIN

Guys! Wang just smoked her first cigarette! Who's next?

The young men all reach for it.

LAI HSIU-CHIN

What the . . . ? Oh, the hell with you—

THE GUYS

Me next! Now me! My turn!

Wang closes her eyes as the bus drifts through the night, indulging herself in the soft rain, while streams of bright streetlights race by.

K'uang comes up and sits beside her.

She turns to him.

K'UANG YU-MIN

Hey.

WANG CHIA-CHIH

Hi.

K'UANG YU-MIN

Thank you—

WANG CHIA-CHIH

For what?

A good-natured, bashful look on K'uang's face. Without saying anything, they look at each other and smile.

Lai Hsiu-chin watches them from her seat in back.

INT. HONG KONG UNIVERSITY AUDITORIUM—DAY

Wang walks out onto the empty, dimly lit stage. It's strewn with pieces of the half-struck set. No one is there.

She stands there, in silence, for a moment.

K'UANG YU-MIN (V.O.—VOICE-OVER)

Wang Chia-chih!

Wang looks up and sees the rest of the group up on the balcony. Lai among them.

LAI HSIU-CHIN

Come on up!

Cut to later, on the balcony, K'uang is holding forth:

K'UANG YU-MIN

I ran into this guy, Tsao De Hsi, the other day, a guy from my hometown in Tsao Ching. He used to hang around the same school as my brother. We go back a long way. I hear that Tsao now works as an assistant to some bigwig in the Peace Movement named Yee.

K'uang keeps his voice very low. The others have to gather close to hear him.

K'UANG YU-MIN

He's one of Wang Ching-wei's lackeys—actually his top agent. Yee is hiding out in Hong Kong now.

HUANG LEI

Wang Ching-wei and his so-called Peace Movement—running dogs for the Japanese! He's a traitor!

K'UANG YU-MIN

That's right. They're recruiting all over the place, and Yee is handling it for him in Hong Kong. What luck I bumped into Tsao—what a chance for us!

A confused silence.

OU-YANG

Uh, a chance for what?

K'uang pauses.

K'UANG YU-MIN

Listen, this is no longer theater club, or shouting slogans. What's wrenching tears from the audience, when we could eliminate a flesh-and-blood traitor! Summer break is coming. We can do some real acting—you change your identities, infiltrate Yee's group. I let Tsao believe I was still friendly with him. Maybe he'll introduce me. We could get some guns . . .

They exchange looks, fearful and excited.

LIANG JUN-SHENG

But what do we know about killing people? Our only experience is onstage!

K'UANG YU-MIN

When you are faced with a real traitor, the killing will come naturally. We should rather worry about how many and how soon we will kill!

And if we're caught, it's the firing squad! So think it through—once you're in, you're in all the way! That's what being young is all about!

HUANG LEI

(slaps his palm on top of K'uang's hand)

I'm in!

OU-YANG

Me too!

(joins his hand with the others)

Huang quietly puts his on the pile.

LAI HSIU-CHIN

Then we must also . . .

K'uang Yu-min

I'm not forcing anyone to join.

Wang Chia-chih

(placing her hand on top)

I'm with you.

Int. Brothel—Hong Kong—Summer 1939—Night

Two prostitutes sit with K'uang, Liang, and Tsao, drinking and playing a drinking game. This scene is all in Cantonese.

Tsao drunkenly puts his arm around K'uang.

Tsao

Say, brother—so good of you to look me up—

K'uang Yu-min

So great to meet up again after all these years away from home. Let's drink to that!

Tsao

Ah, if we can't go home, at least we can meet somebody from home! Bottoms up!

Liang Jun-sheng

Cheers to Brother Tsao! Thanks for looking out for us!

Tsao

I'll see what I can do. Hong Kong's not easy.

> K'UANG YU-MIN

Any chance for me with the organization, brother? I could use some work.

> TSAO

(laughs)

Tough job—I'll see.

EXT. RED LIGHT DISTRICT—HONG KONG—NIGHT

K'uang walks down the narrow stairway, looking upset. He meets Huang Lei, Lai, and Wang on the street. Huang Lei looks back toward the brothel.

> HUANG LEI

Where's Liang?

> K'UANG YU-MIN

Still up there.

> HUANG LEI

What's he doing? We only have enough money to pay for that Tsao guy!

> K'UANG YU-MIN

Maybe he can get more info . . .

They all look back up at the windows of the brothel. Human shadows from the rooms, whores giggling.

HUANG LEI

From them?

INT. SNACK BAR—HONG KONG—SUMMER 1939—DAY

An electric fan twirls. Cantonese music on the radio.

LIANG JUN-SHENG

Tsao said the wives stick to their apartments and play mahjong round the clock.

HUANG LEI

A whole session and that's the only dirt you got?

K'UANG YU-MIN

(*shoots him a dirty look*)

Maybe venturing out is too risky for them, so they don't go out much.

LAI HSIU-CHIN

If they don't come out, what shall we do?

OU-YANG

We should send them a mahjong partner! A fake rich lady to play mahjong in their home—

HUANG LEI

Right! Then lure him out with this pretty lady—

K'uang Yu-min

Stop joking around—

Lai Hsiu-chin

Mahjong—that's beyond me!

K'uang Yu-min

Maybe tomorrow I can get—

Before K'uang can finish, Wang suddenly speaks, very softly.

Wang Chia-chih

I know how to play mahjong! We had mahjong at home. I started playing when I was ten, to make up the foursome!

(smiles)

I've seen how those rich ladies behave at the mahjong table, how they talk . . .

All heads turn to Wang.

Ext. Rented Apartment—Hong Kong—Summer 1939—Day

A car is parked outside an apartment building. The group examines its luxury facade.

Huang Lei

The foreigners have left for the summer. We can rent the second floor for a couple of months.

INT. RENTED APARTMENT—HONG KONG—DAY

Huang opens the door with a key. They enter. K'uang pulls
Huang Lei aside.

K'UANG YU-MIN

Where's all this money coming from?

HUANG LEI

I told you—my old man has a pile stashed in Hong
Kong. He told me I could use it in an emergency!

K'UANG YU-MIN

I never said such a posh place.

HUANG LEI

But you wanted Ou-yang to be Mr. Mai the businessman, with Wang Chia-chih as his rich wife Mai Tai-tai.
Then they have to be living in an apartment like this!

Ou-yang checks out the place.

OU-YANG

A bit of fixing up here, some new furniture there . . .
Lai Hsiu-chin can wear a ponytail and be the
servant . . . And a mustache for Mr. Mai, maybe?

Liang discovers some girlie magazines left behind in the
bathroom.

100

LIANG JUN-SHENG

Ou-yang!

Ou-yang pops in.

LIANG JUN-SHENG

The owner left them!

The two settle down to pore over the magazines. Huang Lei joins them.

EXT. YEE'S RESIDENCE—HONG KONG—SUMMER 1939—DAY

A car pulls up at a gated compound. In the front seat sits Yee's assistant Tsao, next to Huang Lei, who drives, dressed in livery. The car stops. Tsao gets out.

TSAO

(in Cantonese)

Wait here!

Two plainclothes guards exchange signals with Tsao as he enters the compound.

Huang Lei looks in the rearview mirror at Ou-yang. He leans over to straighten Ou-yang's tie.

HUANG LEI

And don't wipe your mouth with it—it's my best tie!

K'uang Yu-min

(seriously)

Stop horsing around! This is not a rehearsal—there are no do-overs! Always remember what role you're playing before opening your mouth! Say only the absolute minimum. The more said, the easier it is to slip!

Wang Chia-chih

You too.

K'uang Yu-min

Here they come!

From the side mirror Wang watches Yee Tai-tai, accompanied by a bodyguard. Both sport dark shades.

K'uang Yu-min opens the door for her.

Tsao

Mr. Mai, Mrs. Mai, and Mr. Mai's cousin K'uang Yu-min, from my hometown!

Yee

Pleased to meet you.

Tsao

This is Mr. Yee, and Yee Tai-tai!

YEE

(to his wife)

Go with them and have fun.

(to the people in the car)

You'll have to excuse me now.

Yee bends slightly to greet everyone, catching a quick glance of Wang. She smiles back at him briefly before he turns to go.

Yee Tai-tai gets inside the car and immediately notices its posh interior.

YEE TAI-TAI

So sorry to bother all of you! You came all this way to fetch me! Tsao told me you knew Hong Kong well, otherwise we could have used my husband's car.

WANG CHIA-CHIH/MAI TAI-TAI

No bother, no bother at all! Would Yee Tai-tai like to shop around Central?

YEE TAI-TAI

After two months in Hong Kong, all I know is Central and Repulse Bay. It's embarrassing!

WANG CHIA-CHIH/MAI TAI-TAI

Then let's go to Tsim Sha Tsui. We can shop there.

YEE TAI-TAI

Okay.

WANG CHIA-CHIH/MAI TAI-TAI

(To Huang Lei, in Cantonese)

To Tsim Sha Tsui!

HUANG LEI

Yes.

Huang Lei starts the car.

WANG CHIA-CHIH/MAI TAI-TAI

(to Ou-yang)

Drop us first and then go back to your office. You wouldn't mind being a little late, would you?

YEE TAI-TAI

We mustn't retain Mr. Mai from his work!

WANG CHIA-CHIH/MAI TAI-TAI

It's all right—it's his family's company!

YEE TAI-TAI

Mr. Mai's line of business is—

OU-YANG

Eh—export!—some import also—

Ou-yang is stuttering. Wang quickly steps in.

WANG CHIA-CHIH/MAI TAI-TAI

You have such a lovely place here, Yee Tai-tai!

(to Ou-yang)

We didn't see this one when we went house hunting.

YEE TAI-TAI

We're only renting. When the war broke out on the Mainland, we had to move here in a hurry. Mai Tai-tai is from Hong Kong?

WANG CHIA-CHIH/MAI TAI-TAI

I came over to get married. My hometown is Kwantung. My mother is from Shanghai.

YEE TAI-TAI

(in Shanghainese)

Then you must know the Shanghai dialect!

WANG CHIA-CHIH/MAI TAI-TAI

(switches to Shanghainese)

Yes, I do, but not very well—I've forgotten most of it!

Yee Tai-tai brightens up at the sound of Shanghainese.

YEE TAI-TAI

(in Shanghainese)

I was originally from Anhui province. My Shanghainese is also so-so!

EXT. DEPARTMENT STORE—HONG KONG—DAY

The two ladies, shaded by their pretty umbrellas, shopping. K'uang follows, two shopping bags in hand.

YEE TAI-TAI

Thank you so much! Sorry to bother you! You are even carrying my things!

K'UANG YU-MIN

No bother—my pleasure!

WANG CHIA-CHIH/MAI TAI-TAI

He's my cousin—it's quite all right! He also arrived in Hong Kong not too long ago. I let him tag along, so he gets to know the place as well.

YEE TAI-TAI

What was your line of business in Kwantung?

K'UANG YU-MIN

I was a teacher—in a village school.

YEE TAI-TAI

No wonder! I thought you looked educated—either a college student, or a teacher!

WANG CHIA-CHIH/MAI TAI-TAI

Yee Tai-tai, you're so observant!

INT. DEPARTMENT STORE—HONG KONG—DAY

Yee Tai-tai picks out a handbag.

YEE TAI-TAI

Very pricey—but the leather is superb!

WANG CHIA-CHIH/MAI TAI-TAI

That price is for foreign customers only. That's Hong Kong for you! Even in the department stores you have to bargain these days. Let me talk to her.

Wang brings the handbag over to bargain with the saleslady.

WANG CHIA-CHIH/MAI TAI-TAI

(in Cantonese)

Excuse me! I'd like to get this

(lowering her voice)

for my aunt, but she won't accept it because it's too expensive! Give me a better price so I can talk her into it!

SALESLADY

(giving her a look)

One hundred and twenty.

WANG CHIA-CHIH/MAI TAI-TAI

Still so high! I know it's imported, but now with the war, the trend is to buy patriotic goods. People would rather not be seen with imported things.

The saleslady knows she's been had.

INT. RENTAL APARTMENT—HONG KONG—SUMMER 1939—NIGHT

The group is sitting, discussing the day's events.

OU-YANG

You see all those plainclothes security? There's no way to get him at the house.

K'UANG YU-MIN

But you saw, when he left, he had a driver and a guard. We'd still have to deal with them, even if we lured him away. It'll take more than one of us shooting.

OU-YANG

That's still got to be better than trying for him at the house—it's an armed camp there.

K'UANG YU-MIN

We just have to be patient. We've made contact—and that Yee Tai-tai has really taken to Wang. She's already asked her back!

Wang Chia-chih stands and turns toward the bedroom.

WANG CHIA-CHIH

Sorry everybody—I'm tired.

She unbuttons her chipao collar as she walks into the bedroom.

K'uang goes to a table and takes out two very old, very clunky handguns and ammo.

K'UANG YU-MIN

Tonight, Huang and Liang will take first shift on guard.

HUANG LEI AND LIANG JUN-SHENG

Of course. No problem.

INT. RENTED APARTMENT—BEDROOM—HONG KONG—NIGHT

LAI HSIU-CHIN (O.S.)

Wang Chia-chih, can I come in?

WANG CHIA-CHIH

Sure.

Wang is carefully taking off her silk stockings as Lai enters, carrying a silk dress.

LAI HSIU-CHIN

I rushed the tailor.

WANG CHIA-CHIH

Thanks.

Wang opens a purse, takes out two cigarettes, and offers one to Lai.

They share a match, sitting on the edge of the bed, smoking in silence.

LAI HSIU-CHIN

This Yee guy, what's he look like?

Wang just shrugs her shoulders, thinking.

WANG CHIA-CHIH

I only caught a quick glimpse. Not exactly what I imagined.

INT. YEE'S RESIDENCE—HONG KONG—SUMMER 1939—NIGHT

The clack of mahjong tiles. Wang plays with Yee Tai-tai and two of her friends, Hsiao Tai-tai and Chu Tai-tai.

HSIAO TAI-TAI

The cook just disappeared on us—just like that! He didn't steal anything, but poof! He just disappeared. It spooked Old Hsiao, though—we haven't set foot in the house in five days, been staying at the Peninsula until they find us another house. He says it isn't safe.

YEE TAI-TAI

You can't trust any of them here. And these Cantonese—they don't understand a word I say!

HSIAO TAI-TAI

What depresses me is there's no one who can cook Shanghainese like that cook. You know how picky that husband of mine is!

WANG CHIA-CHIH/MAI TAI-TAI

There's one restaurant in Hong Kong that has great Shanghainese cuisine. They've got the best drunken chicken, and scallion carp too.

YEE TAI-TAI

Really! You must take us there!

Just then, Yee Tai-tai sees her husband at the doorway.

YEE TAI-TAI

Oh, Old Yee! Mai Tai-tai is just telling us about a real Shanghainese restaurant here.

(to the other women)

He's the picky one! Not even the top restaurants excite him.

He enters the room.

YEE

Oh really? Which one?

YEE TAI-TAI

What's it called again?

WANG CHIA-CHIH/MAI TAI-TAI

(trying to remember)

Chu Jia restaurant—it's in Kowloon, run by the cooks from Tan Jia restaurant in Shanghai.

Yee doesn't seem to take notice of her.

YEE

Yes, I think I've heard of it. (to his wife) I will be out late tonight. Please remember that we are having company tomorrow. Good evening, ladies.

He leaves again.

CHU TAI-TAI

Oh, a party? And why haven't we been invited?

YEE TAI-TAI

(lowering her voice)

He won't even tell me who it is.

HSIAO TAI-TAI

It must be Chen Pi-chun! Wang Ching-wei's wife. They want to set up their own government. Lao Hsiao has also been approached.

> **CHU TAI-TAI**
>
> *(smiles)*

Really! That can only mean one thing—Mr. Yee will be promoted!

> **YEE TAI-TAI**

Aiya!

Yee Tai-tai slams down a tile, smiling like a Cheshire cat.

EXT. YEE'S RESIDENCE—HONG KONG—SUMMER 1939—DAWN

Wang exits the building and walks across the road toward the car.

She taps on the car window and Huang Lei, dressed as a chauffeur, wakes with a start. She gets in and they drive off.

INT. RENTED APARTMENT—HONG KONG—DAY

Huang Lei and Wang enter the apartment, waking the others. K'uang looks worried.

> **K'UANG YU-MIN**

It's late.

> **WANG CHIA-CHIH**

Mahjong. And I lost again.

She walks, exhausted, to the bedroom.

K'UANG YU-MIN

What about Yee? Was he there?

WANG CHIA-CHIH

For a minute. Then he left and never came back.

She takes off her earrings as she goes into the bedroom.
Huang goes to Liang, who is spread out on the couch.

HUANG LEI

Hey, move off. I'm exhausted!

EXT. SEASIDE—HONG KONG—EARLY MORNING

Early morning on a deserted beach. A few gunshots.

K'uang, Huang, and Liang take turns with the two guns, trying
to hit a couple of bottles placed on the rocks in a cove off the
beach. They keep missing. The gun shots set off a chorus of
faraway dogs barking.

Wang and Lai watch them, bored.

Finally, Ou-yang hits a bottle. He's at first startled, then breaks
into a big grin.

OU-YANG

One bottle—assassinated!

HUANG LEI

Hats off to you! It's been a month, and you're so
thrilled about killing a bottle or two. Why don't you
just kill me, and save my old man the trouble!

OU-YANG

Hey—

Huang shrugs off Ou-yang's arm and starts to walk off.

HUANG LEI

Apartment, car, mahjong, expensive shopping . . .

(to Liang)

And your whores. Is this hunting down traitors or
summer camp? How many fathers do I have? Wang
Chia-chih needs her fancy outfits . . .

(to K'uang)

And you need to play resistance hero. What about me?
I'm just a fucking driver by day, and a guard by night.
My father has been asking around, to see if I'm shack-
ing up with some dance girl or something. Now I hear
he wants to disown me. So guess what? You guys are on
your own!

LIANG JUN-SHENG

(to K'uang)

We've got the guns. Why don't we shoot a couple of
easy targets before school starts?

Ou-yang

We all joined of our own free will. Why are you attacking K'uang all of a sudden? This takes patience, and planning . . .

Lai Hsiu-chin

(referring to Wang)

Yes, but if Yee's not hooked he's not hooked! What can you do? You can't just foist yourself upon him!

Ou-yang

You think you'd have a better chance?

Lai's eyes spit fire.

K'uang Yu-min

You're right about the money—if anyone, I should have foreseen the consequences. And let's face it, we're amateurs. But we've spent all this time and effort. We have access to Yee. Are we going to give up now? I know the guards now. Maybe I should just go do it, and take the consequences myself.

Huang Lei

Don't be silly. You think you can survive getting to that Yee guy on your own?

K'UANG YU-MIN

That's my business!

He turns and walks away. Huang runs up and grabs him.

HUANG LEI

Listen, I was just letting off steam. Summer's almost over. I was just worried that time is running out on us.

OU-YANG

(*relieved*)

All right. Let's head back, guys.

EXT. YEE'S RESIDENCE—HONG KONG—SUMMER 1939

An afternoon rainstorm.

Wang gets out of a taxi and runs in small steps toward Yee's residence. Her umbrella flips in the wind.

A black umbrella opens in front of the main entrance. Mr. Yee stands beneath it, talking to his assistant.

YEE

The papers are in my study.

Yee sees Wang approaching. She takes shelter under his umbrella.

WANG CHIA-CHIH/MAI TAI-TAI

Oh, Mr. Yee!

Yee looks at her wet face and wet hair. He smiles.

YEE

Mai Tai-tai!

WANG CHIA-CHIH/MAI TAI-TAI

My car broke down halfway, then this rain.

Without speaking, Yee takes a handkerchief from his pocket and gives it to her to dry her face.

He stands with her for a moment under the umbrella.

YEE

(to his assistant)

Accompany Mai Tai-tai inside.

The door opens behind them, and Tsao comes out with a packet of papers. Yee takes them and gets into the car, as Wang goes inside.

INT. YEE'S RESIDENCE—HONG KONG—SUMMER 1939

The downpour continues.

Yee Tai-tai, Wang, and Chu Tai-tai sit languidly, bored.

YEE TAI-TAI

Hong Kong is so humid! You can squeeze water out just by making a fist!

WANG CHIA-CHIH/MAI TAI-TAI

I must say Shanghai is not quite as bad. After all these years, I'm still not used to it here.

They hear the sound of the door.

YEE TAI-TAI

(*yells*)

Aiya, Chu Tai-tai, finally!—I thought you'd never come with this typhoon outside!

But it turns out to be Mr. Yee. He brushes the water off his clothes.

YEE TAI-TAI

Ah, you're back so soon?

YEE

The storm—my appointment's been canceled. Ah, I see Mai Tai-tai and Chu Tai-tai are here.

YEE TAI-TAI

We were waiting for Chu Tai-tai. And you're just in time! We need a fourth for mahjong!

YEE

I can't—too much paperwork.

YEE TAI-TAI

Come, just this once! Old Yee, when was the last time you played?

CHU TAI-TAI

(chipping in)

Come on! Look how sweet Yee Tai-tai is with you!

YEE

Well, if you insist.

Later:

The storm rages outside, almost a typhoon.

The four of them are in the middle of a game.

YEE

Bei.

CHU TAI-TAI

Bei.

YEE

Chiwong.

WANG CHIA-CHIH/MAI TAI-TAI

Chi. Dongfun.

Wang takes a tile discarded by Yee, fiddling with it innocently. Yee is letting her have it, she knows, but is pretending not to notice.

YEE TAI-TAI

The fabric we got the other day? My husband actually likes it! But he wants to change the tailor—know of anyone good?

WANG CHIA-CHIH/MAI TAI-TAI

Yes I do. They're good at both chipao and Western suits. We all go there.

YEE

Nan.

CHU TAI-TAI

Pung.

YEE TAI-TAI

Shall we try them? Old Yee could use a couple of new suits, couldn't you?

YEE

Whatever you say.

He focuses on the tiles before him.

> YEE

Chitong.

> WANG CHIA-CHIH/MAI TAI-TAI

Chi.

> YEE TAI-TAI

Pung.

> WANG CHIA-CHIH/MAI TAI-TAI

But they're awfully busy with the tourists right now.

> YEE TAI-TAI

It's not going to take months, is it?

> WANG CHIA-CHIH/MAI TAI-TAI

No. I'm an old customer. I can tell them to do you first.

> YEE

Chitong.

> WANG CHIA-CHIH/MAI TAI-TAI

Chi. Chitong.

> *(takes out a notepad to write)*

Why don't we do this—when Mr. Yee has a moment, just give me a ring, all right, Yee Tai-tai?

She tears off the paper with her phone number on it.

YEE TAI-TAI

Mai Tai-tai, I have your number!

Wang leaves the paper in a nearby cake dish.

WANG CHIA-CHIH/MAI TAI-TAI

Pung. Shutiu.

YEE TAI-TAI

When the sales are on, let's go and get more material!

WANG CHIA-CHIH/MAI TAI-TAI

I can tell Mr. Yee likes imported English wool. Too bad it never really goes on sale.

YEE

Is that so?

Yee puts aside a tile he's been fiddling with for a while. He takes a piece of cake and glances at the phone number.

Then casually he discards the tile.

It's Wang's turn. Just as casually she picks up the discarded tile.

WANG CHIA-CHIH/MAI TAI-TAI

(looks at the tile with slight astonishment,
then breaks into a wide smile)

Aiya! Does this mean I won?

She flips over the tiles and glances at Yee Tai-tai.

YEE TAI-TAI

Well, you're lucky today!

WANG CHIA-CHIH/MAI TAI-TAI

Really! The god of fortune is indeed here today!

INT. RENTED APARTMENT—HONG KONG—DAY

A gramophone plays loud dance music, as Ou-yang and
Lai Hsiu-chin show off some fancy dance steps to the
gang.

The telephone rings. Wang picks it up.

WANG CHIA-CHIH

Hello? . . . Oh, It's you. . . . Of course I recognized your
voice.

The group quiets down. K'uang quickly switches off the music.
All look at Wang.

INT. TAILOR SHOP—HONG KONG—DAY

A tailor drapes a jacket on Yee.

He stands in front of the mirror, with Wang next to him. Both are reflected in the mirror.

WANG CHIA-CHIH/MAI TAI-TAI

(in Cantonese)

The collar can be a little more snug.

TAILOR

Okay. Looks better with the smaller collar.

WANG CHIA-CHIH/MAI TAI-TAI

And the sleeves a little bit shorter.

Wang notices him looking at her in the mirror, and blushes slightly.

WANG CHIA-CHIH/MAI TAI-TAI

(to Yee)

The shorter sleeves look more energetic.

YEE

Whatever you say. I'm in your hands.

WANG CHIA-CHIH/MAI TAI-TAI

It's the latest look—a close-fitting collar.

The tailor notes the corrections. Another assistant comes forward with a beautiful chipao.

TAILOR

Ah, madam. We've made the alterations. Please.

WANG CHIA-CHIH/MAI TAI-TAI

I'll be right back.

The assistant leads her behind a changing area behind a curtain.

Yee walks toward the door and hands some money over to Tsao.

YEE

Go get lunch. Don't wait for me.

TSAO

Yes.

Yee returns to the tailor.

YEE

Mai Tai-tai must be a very good customer.

The tailor looks confused—perhaps it takes him a beat to understand Yee's Mandarin.

TAILOR

(in Cantonese)

Hmmm? . . . Oh yes, very good, very good.

Wang walks back into the room in her new dress.

Wang Chia-chih/Mai Tai-tai

(in Cantonese)

Perhaps you took in a bit too much this time. I can
hardly breathe!

Wang walks back and forth, showing off her slender body
sheathed in the snug chipao. Yee studies her.

Wang Chia-chih/Mai Tai-tai

Yee Tai-tai actually picked this one first, and then
decided against it. She said it made her skin look
sallow. So I took it for myself.

(checks her profile in the mirror)

Hmm. I suppose it's fine as is. Let me go and change.

Yee

(quietly)

No. Leave it on.

Wang hesitates—a moment of confusion, then triumph, as it
sinks in.

Wang Chia-chih/Mai Tai-tai

Of course.

Int. Private Club at Repulse Bay—Hong Kong—Day

Exclusive. The only other diners are three elderly English ladies
at a faraway table. Yee speaks on the phone in a booth near the

entrance to the restaurant, while Wang sits and waits for him at a table, dressed in the new chipao.

> YEE

All right.

Yee puts down the phone and goes to the table.

> WANG CHIA-CHIH/MAI TAI-TAI

Nothing serious, I hope! Yee Tai-tai—

> YEE

Tsao's taken her to the doctor's. She complained of a headache as she was leaving. I guess it's all that mahjong.

> WANG CHIA-CHIH/MAI TAI-TAI

Little Mai doesn't like my playing either. We often argue about it. I told him men have endless outside distractions while we ladies have only shopping and mahjong. You'd think mahjong should be okay. At least it keeps us at home!

Yee smiles and takes a good look at Wang.

> YEE

I hope I didn't interrupt anything when I called today. . . .

WANG CHIA-CHIH/MAI TAI-TAI

Little Mai is away in Singapore, so his friends came over to keep me company.

(*laughs*)

More like to keep an eye on me. Your call gave me the perfect excuse to leave.

YEE

Is that right?

Later, dinner is in progress.

WANG CHIA-CHIH/MAI TAI-TAI

Sometimes I don't mind doing things on my own. Little Mai and I don't much like the same things.

YEE

What do you like?

WANG CHIA-CHIH/MAI TAI-TAI

Going to the movies. Little Mai won't go with me, so I go by myself. He and his friends only talk business. They don't like movies.

YEE

I don't go to the movies either.

> #### WANG CHIA-CHIH/MAI TAI-TAI
>
> Mr. Yee, you are too busy. Movies are for people with time to kill.

> #### YEE
>
> No, it's not that. You see, I don't like the dark.

Wang gives Yee a quizzical look.

> #### YEE
>
> Would you like a drink?

> #### WANG CHIA-CHIH/MAI TAI-TAI
>
> I'll have a little to keep you company.

Yee pours her some brandy.

> #### YEE
>
> You've been so kind to us here in Hong Kong—we know very few people.

> #### WANG CHIA-CHIH/MAI TAI-TAI
>
> Oh please—such trivial things!

> #### YEE
>
> But if you pay attention, nothing is trivial.

Wang sips her brandy. Yee takes in the kiss of lipstick on the glass rim.

Wang looks around and finds no other diners.

WANG CHIA-CHIH/MAI TAI-TAI

How come nobody comes here?

YEE

Because the food is so bad.

Wang puts down her fork and knife.

YEE

(chuckles)

My apologies! But it's a perfect place to talk, for no one is here to disturb you. . . . Your husband, he works a great deal?

WANG CHIA-CHIH/MAI TAI-TAI

For what, I have no idea. He's always away in Singapore or somewhere on business. But as they say, a man is fine as long as he's not in the house.

(asks smilingly)

True?

Yee smiles.

YEE

And what does he do there?

131

Wang Chia-chih/Mai Tai-tai

(flirtatious)

Why are you so interested in my husband? If he's so fascinating to you, maybe I should bring him along next time? You men have so much to say to each other, but with women, you just make small talk!

Yee

(laughs)

Small talk like this—you have no idea—it's a luxury for me.

The lights dim. Waiters start placing candles on the tables.

Yee

I listen to men all day, so-called prominent politicians and the like, talking their supposed serious talk. And you know what? No matter what high-sounding words come out of their mouths, I see only one thing in their eyes.

Wang Chia-chih/Mai Tai-tai

And what's that?

Yee

Fear. But you . . . for some reason, you don't seem afraid. . . . Are you?

Wang keeps her smile.

WANG CHIA-CHIH/MAI TAI-TAI

How about you?

YEE

You're smart, but not so smart at mahjong.

WANG CHIA-CHIH/MAI TAI-TAI

You're right. I always lose. Except when you let me win.

With a smile, Yee lights a cigarette.

WANG CHIA-CHIH/MAI TAI-TAI

May I—

Yee passes her a cigarette. The two move closer together. Yee lights the cigarette for her.

EXT/INT. TAXI—HONG KONG—NIGHT

Wang and Yee sit in the back of a cab. A slightly awkward silence.

WANG CHIA-CHIH/MAI TAI-TAI

I'll pick up your suit when it's ready, or—

YEE

I'll call you.

Again silence. Yee takes another look at Wang.

YEE

Unfortunately, I have another appointment this
evening. I still have a bit of time, though. Allow me to
drop you off first. . . . You don't mind?

WANG CHIA-CHIH/MAI TAI-TAI

Of course not.

EXT. RENTED APARTMENT—HONG KONG—NIGHT

Liang is keeping watch on the balcony, when he sees the taxi
pull up and stop in front of the building. He sees Wang and Yee
in the back, still talking.

He makes a mad dash inside.

INT. RENTED APARTMENT—HONG KONG—NIGHT

LIANG JUN-SHENG

They're here!

K'UANG YU-MIN

Lights off! Go out and keep an eye on them.

Lai quickly turns the lights out.

K'uang and Ou-yang run for their guns.

EXT. RENTED APARTMENT—HONG KONG—NIGHT

Yee gets out of the taxi, comes around, and opens the door for
Wang.

WANG CHIA-CHIH/MAI TAI-TAI

Thank you.

YEE

Please, I will see you to the door.

WANG CHIA-CHIH/MAI TAI-TAI

You really shouldn't bother.

Yee hands some money to the driver, asking him to stay and wait for him, then walks with Wang up the driveway toward the apartment.

WANG CHIA-CHIH/MAI TAI-TAI

Fine with me. It's your appointment—just don't blame me if you're late.

INT. RENTED APARTMENT—HONG KONG—CONTINUOUS

K'uang cocks his gun and stands in the corridor beside the door.

Ou-yang, gun in hand, presses with the others against the wall in the living room.

EXT. RENTED APARTMENT—HONG KONG—CONTINUOUS

Wang takes her keys from her purse. She turns and leans against the door. With her eyes trained on him, she slowly spreads the keys out in her hand, picks out the right one, turns and thrusts it into the keyhole. Yee watches. With a click, the door is unlocked.

135

WANG CHIA-CHIH/MAI TAI-TAI

You and your appointment—otherwise—you could
send the cab away and come in—for a cup of tea.

Wang twists her body around to look at Yee.

Yee smiles warmly.

INT. RENTAL APARTMENT—HONG KONG—AUTUMN 1939— NIGHT

In the dark, all eyes are fixed on the door. We hear the muffled
sounds of footsteps.

Then, silence.

The sound of the key in the door.

The door to the apartment opens slowly. We see Wang's
silhouette as light from the hallway spills into the apartment.

K'uang aims the pistol.

Wang closes the door behind her. It is pitch-dark.

She flips on the light. It's just her. The group is backed up
against the walls. K'uang's hand shakes—the pistol is still
pointed at her.

She takes it all in.

WANG CHIA-CHIH

I need a drink.

Later:

A few drinks later, everyone is topsy-turvy on the sofas or
sitting on the floor, peanut shells all over the place.

Wang Chia-chih

He's so cautious that he sent Tsao and the bodyguard away the minute he got to the tailors! He trusts no one, and that includes Tsao.

Huang Lei

Simple! Next time you do just like today, and when you get him to come inside, we'll finish him off with one shot!

Wang Chia-chih

He would never come in—that I know. He probably keeps some secret apartments, hideaways for just this kind of thing. Maybe even Tsao has no idea.

Ou-yang

Did he try anything?

Huang Lei slaps Ou-yang on the back.

Huang Lei

Hey, Mr. Mai is jealous!

Wang Chia-chih

(lowers her voice)

I knew what was on his mind. Otherwise he wouldn't have seen me to the door. Only he didn't dare come in, but he kept me for a good long while. . . .

Wang's mind wanders off for a few moments. She sips her drink.

WANG CHIA-CHIH

(pretty drunk, almost to herself)

He said he'd call again. I wanted to lure him into a theater, where it's easier for you guys to get away—but he's so cautious he won't go into dark places! When he calls again, then he'll be serious. Then I'll have him hooked. I'll be his mistress. But what shall I do? We have to think now. We have to think what we're going to do with him.

There's an awkward silence. K'uang gets up and goes to the balcony. One by one, the boys follow suit, Liang being the last to go, until Wang is left with Lai.

Lai turns to her.

LAI HSIU-CHIN

Would you know—what to do . . .

Wang looks at her.

LAI HSIU-CHIN

What to do with a man?

Wang is silent. For a good while. She lifts her head and sees the boys smoking on the balcony.

WANG CHIA-CHIH

So, you've already discussed it.

LAI HSIU-CHIN

Hm.

WANG CHIA-CHIH

Which one?

LAI HSIU-CHIN

Liang is the only one with experience.

WANG CHIA-CHIH

With whores, you mean.

Lai Hsiu-chin nods.

Wang is silent.

Wang gets up and regards the boys outside. A bit unsteadily, she walks back toward the bedroom.

INT. RENTED APARTMENT—BEDROOM—HONG KONG— NIGHT

Wang enters the room and looks at herself in the mirror.

Slowly, she begins to undress, watching herself the whole time.

With the last of her clothes off, she goes to the bed and gets under the covers.

The bedroom door opens, and Liang enters, bottle and glasses in hand.

LIANG JUN-SHENG

Want a drink?

WANG CHIA-CHIH

No.

He takes a big sip and puts the bottle on the nightstand. Nervously, he begins to unbutton his shirt and sits on the edge of the bed.

WANG CHIA-CHIH

The light.

He turns off the light, finishes undressing, and then gets under the covers.

In the dark, we hear only his heavy breathing. Wang's eyes glow. He reaches down to feel her but she pushes his hand away. Wang gasps and flinches as he quickly enters her. After a moment of panic, Liang settles in to a grim, mechanical rhythm.

INT. RENTAL APARTMENT—HONG KONG—MORNING

Lai dries her hair on the balcony.

K'uang and Huang Lei set the table for breakfast.

Wang comes out of the bedroom.

She walks toward the bathroom, pauses, looking perfectly normal.

WANG CHIA-CHIH

I need to use the bathroom—anyone else . . .

No one says anything. Lai watches from the balcony.

Ou-yang quickly gathers his sudsy clothes and cedes the bathroom to her. He goes into the kitchen to continue his laundry.

Wang goes inside the bathroom and closes the door.

K'uang looks up. A moment later he sees Wang exit the bathroom and return to the bedroom, firmly shutting the door behind her.

INT. RENTED APARTMENT—BEDROOM—DAY

Thick drapes block out the sun.

Liang and Wang are in bed, Wang on top, mechanically riding him.

LIANG JUN-SHENG

I think you're starting to get the hang of it.

WANG CHIA-CHIH

Leave me alone.

She keeps at it.

Later:

Wang lies, alone, in the bed.

She gets up and goes over to the window, pulling open the drapes.

A sprig of bright green ivy pokes its head against the windowpane, translucent against the afternoon sun.

Int. Rented Apartment—Hong Kong—Afternoon

K'uang goes over to Wang's bedroom door, hesitates, then knocks.

> #### K'uang Yu-min
>
> Wang Chia-chih—

Behind the door Wang is making up her eyebrows.

> #### K'uang Yu-min
>
> Time to eat.

K'uang's voice is feeble. He looks awful.

> #### Wang Chia-chih
>
> I'm not hungry.

> #### K'uang Yu-min
>
> We cooked congee.

Just then, we hear the phone ring. Wang jumps up and dashes out of the bedroom. Ignoring the others, she grabs the phone breathlessly.

WANG CHIA-CHIH

Hello! Ah, it's you, Yee Tai-tai! I called you a couple of days ago, but you were out. I wanted to ask if you wanted to get your dress made? No? Why?

Wang's face darkens.

WANG CHIA-CHIH

Moving back to Shanghai? . . . My congratulations to both of you! How about I come by? I can be there right now! Haven't heard from you for so many days, I was going to drop by anyway! Then I'll go to the airport tomorrow—

(*sounding confused*)

I should at least treat you to a farewell dinner!... You're not leaving just like this? I . . . I . . . Oh well . . . okay . . . please give my regards to Mr. Yee. Have a safe trip. Good-bye!

Wang hangs up and sits there, red lips slightly quivering. Everyone stares at her.

INT. RENTED APARTMENT—HONG KONG—NIGHT

Lai climbs up to take down the curtains. Rental furnishings are stacked in one corner, trash in another.

Wang sits alone, motionless, at the table. The others move back and forth in front of her, methodically packing and moving things. No one asks her to help; no one looks at her.

Wang gets up and steps out the french doors onto the balcony. She lights a cigarette with a practiced hand.

At first neither she, nor anyone else in the group, notices a figure slipping into the apartment and standing, his hands in his pockets, at the front door.

He kicks the door closed behind him. Everyone stops at the sound of the door slamming.

It's Tsao, looking around the room, grinning.

Tsao

Moving out? I hope I'm not disturbing you guys.

He lets out a little laugh. The group senses danger.

Tsao

(to Huang Lei)

Little Huang, no longer a driver? Instead he's become a mover?

K'uang Yu-min

Tsao! What brings you here?

Tsao

Just thought I'd give my regards to Mr. Mai, and Mrs. Mai, and all the little Mai children. How cute you all are!

K'uang Yu-min

What are you getting at?

TSAO

I had my suspicions from the start. But I kept my peace until I could see what your game was.

(nodding toward Ou-yang, who is wearing a Lingnan University T-shirt)

So Mr. Mai is from Lingnan U?

K'UANG YU-MIN

You don't know what you're talking about.

TSAO

Oh yeah? Then how's this? You see, Yee just fired me. So it's time for me to switch sides. I think the people you're working for would find me very valuable.

K'UANG YU-MIN

How much do you want?

TSAO

Hmmm. How about ten taels of gold, for five heads?

(sees Wang on the balcony)

And that's not counting Mai Tai-tai. I'd expect a premium for her from Mr. Yee!

K'UANG YU-MIN

You wouldn't dare!

Tsao

You're something else, brother! I had no idea you were
a secret agent! Why didn't you help me instead of using
me, huh? After all, we're from the same village!

We cut to Wang, still standing outside, watching the figures in
the harsh shadows cast by the lamplights. Through the glass
doors, she hears the muffled sounds of conversation. She sees,
from behind, K'uang's hand slowly reaching toward the dish
rack for a knife.

Suddenly, as K'uang makes a move for the knife, Tsao pulls a
pistol.

K'uang Yu-min

Tsao!

Wang's POV, her terrified face fleetingly reflected in the glass:

There's a scream from Lai, Ou-yang leaps and pushes Tsao, the
dull thud of a gunshot, an inchoate struggle as a lamp falls and
the gang leaps on Tsao, trying to pull the gun from his hands,
punching and kicking. The action is almost comical, pathetic,
but desperate.

Tsao rolls over and stands, trying to finger the trigger of his
gun, as K'uang runs to him and, with all his might, plunges the
knife into his stomach.

Wang pulls open the door and takes a step inside, as everyone
else steps back from Tsao, stunned, silent.

Tsao looks down at the knife in his stomach.

Amazingly Tsao, with great pain, pulls the knife out of his stomach. As he holds it up, Ou-yang grabs his arm. Liang takes the knife and slashes Tsao with it. Blood sprays them all. As they recoil, Tsao stumbles to the door and tries to pry it open, leaving a trail of blood.

The group follows him, watching, not quite knowing what to do.

He fumbles with the handle and starts to bellow in pain.

TSAO

(painfully)

You!

K'UANG YU-MIN

You worked for a traitor. You should know what was coming!

Liang finally rushes after Tsao with the knife and stabs him in the back, as Tsao falls to his knees. Liang trips over him and tumbles a few steps, now covered in blood.

LAI HSIU-CHIN

(trembling)

He's still alive.

Tsao still bellows like a pig. K'uang now goes to Tsao and clumsily tries to break his neck. After a few tries, there's a crack—then silence. He's done it.

147

We hear Lai, wild-eyed, swallowing her screams. Everyone is panting, hardly able to take in the horrifying scene.

Wang looks at all of them, each one in shock.

Slowly, she walks to the door, steps over Tsao's body, opens the door, and leaves.

No one says a word.

She doesn't look back.

Ext. Rented Apartment—Hong Kong—Night

She steps out into the night.

We stay on her face—impassive, traumatized—as she slowly walks down the hill and away.

Fade out.

TITLE: Three Years Later

Ext. Shanghai Street—Early Morning

A bird's-eye view of Shanghai, 1942. The Wai Bai Du Bridge checkpoint, a rising sun in the distant morning.

Off the Bund, a neat row of tricycles, men off to work during the morning rush hour. Two corpses in suits are sprawled on the bloodstained street. A policeman stands guard. People pass by with barely a glance, as a group of White Russian prostitutes in shabby attire solicit from among the throng.

Ext. Food Store in Alley—Shanghai—Spring— Early Morning

The store is not yet open. Outside there is already a long line of people, of all looks and ages. They have been standing in line the whole night.

Wang Chia-chih, expressionless, is among them, her head lowered. Her clothes are flimsy and half her face is hidden behind a head scarf. She looks tired, her innocence long lost.

The wooden shutters of the food store finally are removed. The line begins to stir.

Later: it's Wang's turn in front of the counter. She picks up a small sack of low-quality rice. Quickly she turns and walks away, passing by homeless people lying around on the streets. Sanitation workers lift up an emaciated corpse into a cart.

Ext. Shanghai Streets—Morning

Wang turns into an alley, passing by people with their night soil buckets to dump into the waiting cart. At the entrance to her building, someone is stoking a coal-fired stove, sending off thick clouds of white smoke. Wang pushes open the back door and enters into the communal kitchen. She pours the rice into her family container and locks it. Then she walks upstairs.

Int. Wang's Aunt's House—Shanghai—Day

Wang opens the door with a key and hears mahjong playing inside. Someone from the third floor greets her.

NEIGHBOR

Good morning.

WANG CHIA-CHIH

Good morning.

Mechanically, she closes the door.

A cramped space with good redwood furniture, betraying a once-glorious past. Two rooms are squeezed out of this tiny space, one of which has in the middle a mahjong table with four players. The table is padded with a thick material, to minimize the noise.

WANG CHIA-CHIH

It's me, Aunt.

A middle-aged woman focusing on her tiles turns her head to look at her.

AUNT

Any mail from your father?

WANG CHIA-CHIH

I'll check later.

She goes into her room, picks up some books, and readies to leave again.

WANG CHIA-CHIH

I'm off to class!

150

MAHJONG PARTNER

(a glance at the aunt)

You still let her go to school?

AUNT

I sold the big house left her by her father! I promised to let her finish school. I'm one who keeps her word!

The aunt, cigarette in mouth and a jade bangle on her wrist, juggles her tiles unhurriedly. From her looks and style, we can tell that she once lived a life of luxury.

INT. LECTURE ROOM—SHANGHAI UNIVERSITY—DAY

Simple words in Japanese are written on the blackboard. A Japanese teacher in kimono gives lessons to a poorly attended class, Wang among them.

EXT. MEICHI CINEMA—SHANGHAI—DAY

Wang stands in front of a movie poster. She pauses, reaches into her pocket, and finds enough money to buy a ticket.

INT. MEICHI CINEMA—SHANGHAI—DAY

Wang watches the movie in the crowded cinema.

Suddenly, the movie is interrupted by a Japanese war newsreel, full of images of Sino-Japanese friendship. Everyone begins to chat and get up, ignoring the newsreel.

AUDIENCE MEMBER

I'm going to the bathroom.

INT. MEICHI CINEMA LOBBY—SHANGHAI—NIGHT

Wang walks down the stairs, crosses the lobby, and heads for the entrance.

From a corner of the lobby, someone is watching her. It's Lai Hsiu-chin.

EXT. WANG'S AUNT'S HOUSE—SHANGHAI—MORNING

Wang comes out of the house.

As she reaches the street, she bumps into someone. Looking up, she's shocked to discover K'uang in front of her—older, thinner, almost haunted looking.

INT. SMALL TEAHOUSE—SHANGHAI—EARLY SPRING 1942—DAY

Wang and K'uang sit in the upper floor of a small teahouse.

K'UANG YU-MIN

We've all been through a lot.

WANG CHIA-CHIH

I didn't expect you to be still alive.

K'UANG YU-MIN

I should be dead, if not for . . .

(pauses)

You never knew, did you?

WANG CHIA-CHIH

What?

K'UANG YU-MIN

In Hong Kong, we were being watched the whole time. That night, after you left, they came and took care of the mess, and smuggled us out of Hong Kong.

WANG CHIA-CHIH

Who were they?

K'UANG YU-MIN

The "Blue Shirts," from Chungking! The same ones who were responsible for the assassination of the mayor of Shanghai, Fu Xiao An, the chief detective, Lu Yun Kui, and even the minister for foreign affairs, Chen Lu! Now you know—how absurd we were! How childish!

WANG CHIA-CHIH

Especially me—how naive I was!

K'UANG YU-MIN

It was all my fault.

WANG CHIA-CHIH

We've all paid our dues. How is everybody?

K'UANG YU-MIN

They're all still alive.

153

WANG CHIA-CHIH

Where are they?

K'UANG YU-MIN

Somewhere, I'm not supposed to say. I have been looking for you.

A pause.

WANG CHIA-CHIH

After what happened, I didn't go back to university. I went to teach at a language school. It was like I lost all my memories. My father wrote and said he couldn't afford to bring me to England. He sent me to Shanghai to stay with my aunt. These past years I've felt so empty, so hollow . . .

(smiles weakly)

So I insist on taking classes, even Japanese!

K'UANG YU-MIN

I'm glad you've gone back to school. That, to me, is closed forever.

It dawns on Wang that her bumping into K'uang was not accidental.

WANG CHIA-CHIH

So you've tracked me down—just to say you're sorry?

K'uang Yu-min

There's a mission.

(in a low voice)

The job we all started with, it's still unfinished. Yee is now in charge of Wang Ching-wei's secret service, really just a watchdog for the Japanese. He murders judges, professors, journalists, and our agents. We missed our chance three years ago—that was a bitter lesson. Now it's even more difficult, for he's well protected. We can't get to him.

Wang Chia-chih

And so you bumped into me?

Ext. Sunrise Bookstore—Shanghai—Day

To establish: an old derelict neighborhood, watch repairmen and medicine men hawking their wares.

Piles of old books and magazines are stacked in front of a small bookstore.

K'uang is acquiring some used books by weight from an old man. Wang approaches.

K'uang pays the seller and adds the books to a pile.

Old Man

Hey boss, come on, you can do better than that.

K'uang gives him a few more coins.

K'UANG YU-MIN

(to Wang Chia-chih)

Come with me.

(to some kids looking around the store)

Don't touch anything.

INT. SUNRISE BOOKSTORE—SHANGHAI—DAY

K'uang leads Wang into the back of the bookstore. She notices Ou-yang and Liang from her old Hong Kong days, busily stacking books. They see her, too, but avert their eyes.

K'UANG YU-MIN

Chia-chih, this way.

Up some old steps in the back. K'uang gives two short knocks.

The door opens, and Old Wu, a middle-aged man with a hint of dangerous cynicism, greets them, giving Wang a quick once-over.

OLD WU

Ah, Miss Wang, what a pleasure to meet you, finally! So much to do, of course, so little time. We'll start from the beginning, but please do sit! I trust K'uang has already briefed you? Yes, so can we get straight to the point? Are you ready?

Wang nods, eyes trained on Old Wu.

OLD WU

Good. First things first, but also the last! Before you go on your mission, you'll sew this into your clothes.

He takes out a tiny capsule.

OLD WU

In case you're caught.

K'UANG YU-MIN

(soothingly)

Just in case.

OLD WU

(eyes on Wang)

It will not be too painful, but you must move fast, before anyone gets to your hands, yes?

Wang nods. Old Wu closely monitors her every reaction.

OLD WU

You have a good memory, yes? I'm going to tell you many things, and you must keep them in your head. Repeat them, until they sink in. Don't ask, don't think, just remember everything, got it? You are Mai Tai-tai, you have no relatives any more in Shanghai—you must remember this, important point. For our enemy, I'm afraid, has become even more distrustful and cunning.

Once he becomes suspicious, you'll be finished! I must warn you of that right now!

WANG CHIA-CHIH

I can do it.

Old Wu hands her a file.

OLD WU

This is your personal file. You married Mr. Mai four years ago. This is your marriage license, your anniversary date . . .

As Old Wu continues, we go into a montage of Wang's training and preparation.

A tailor takes her measurements.

An agent shows Wang how to pick locks.

K'uang Yu-min teaches her how to load a pistol.

OLD WU (V.O.)

You moved from Garden Road to Johnston Road, and had to become a runner to help out after Hong Kong fell and business went bad for Little Mai—here's your home phone, husband's business phone, some Hong Kong prices, your bank account number, ah yes, so many things to remember! Answer everything without hesitation—that's step number one! Once you're on, there's no turning back, got it?

Wang bids farewell to her aunt, suitcase in hand.

INT. SUNRISE BOOKSTORE—STOREROOM—SHANGHAI— DAY

Old Wu and K'uang wait for Wang. Old Wu is dressed in a business suit.

Wang enters. Old Wu gestures to a couple of expensive-looking suitcases.

Wang opens a suitcase, her hand lightly touching the finery inside, the cartons of cigarettes and packages of medicine.

OLD WU

Go through your luggage—stockings, medicines— remember their prices. My part is over, now it's your show. Any questions?

WANG CHIA-CHIH

I wrote my father a letter. Please—after you read it— post it for me.

She hands the letter to Old Wu. He nods.

OLD WU

After the mission, we'll send you to England to join your father! All right, now go behind that curtain and change. I'd like to meet Mai Tai-tai.

She takes a chipao and goes to a dressing area in the corner of the room, behind a curtain.

OLD WU

(to K'uang)

Is everything ready on your end?

K'UANG YU-MIN

The car is ready. The hotel, we've paid for one week in advance. Wang Ching-wei's people all meet up there. Yee Tai-tai goes there often, so they are bound to run into each other.

While listening, Old Wu reads Wang's letter. Then he burns it and throws it into the bin.

K'uang keeps quiet—he expected this—but he's almost sickened by the offhand cruelty of it.

Wang pulls the curtain back.

She's transformed—the very image of Shanghai beauty. Old Wu holds out his hand, holding a ring.

OLD WU

Your wedding band.

Wang stretches out her hand. She already has one on.

WANG CHIA-CHIH

My mother's ring, the one I wore three years ago. I'd better keep the same one.

Old Wu smiles.

OLD WU

Mai Tai-tai, pleased to meet you!

INT. LIVING ROOM AT YEE'S RESIDENCE—SHANGHAI—WINTER 1942—NIGHT

Yee comes home, exhausted and preoccupied. Though more withdrawn and gaunt-looking than in Hong Kong, his eyes remain as piercing as ever.

His assistant Chang follows behind, a dossier in hand.

The usual mahjong clatter.

Yee walks quietly upstairs.

YEE TAI-TAI (V.O.)

Let Mai Tai-tai know what you need and she'll bring it over from Hong Kong.

Yee stops at these words.

YEE

Wait for me in the study—I'll be right there.

CHANG

Yes, sir.

Chang nods and continues on.

Yee stays and listens.

YEE TAI-TAI (V.O.)

What a coincidence. I went with Liao Tai-tai to have dinner at the Great East Asia Hotel and bumped into her! She's been back and forth to Shanghai, and we never knew!

MAI TAI-TAI/WANG CHIA-CHIH (V.O.)

It's really my fault. I should have looked you up long ago, but my husband has kept me so busy with business here.

YEE TAI-TAI (V.O.)

We have so many extra rooms. Why waste money staying in a hotel?

Yee turns and walks into the mahjong chamber.

LIAO TAI-TAI

Ah, Hong Kong—haven't been there for a while!

Looking into the mahjong chamber, Yee studies Wang as she pulls up a stool next to Yee Tai-tai to watch the game. He watches her in silence for a moment.

YEE TAI-TAI

Ah, there you are! Look who's here. You remember Mai Tai-tai, from Hong Kong?

Yee nods and smiles, warmly.

MAI TAI-TAI/WANG CHIA-CHIH

How are you, Mr. Yee? I'm sure you don't remember me.

YEE

Of course I do. How is Mr. Mai? How's business?

MAI TAI-TAI/WANG CHIA-CHIH

Thanks for asking—difficult.

(to Yee Tai-tai)

Mr. Yee seems to have lost some weight.

Ma Tai-tai, one of the ladies at the mahjong table, looks Wang in the eyes, studying her.

YEE TAI-TAI

I did ask him to think twice before accepting his post—you pay with your life, and have to step on so many toes!

YEE

Stepping on others' toes is all right, but not on my wife's!

YEE TAI-TAI

(laughing)

Off with you!

YEE

All right—you ladies continue.

With this and a smile Yee leaves.

He heads for the study, looking back once.

In the mahjong room, the discussion continues.

LIAO TAI-TAI (V.O.)

Listen to him, what a gentleman!

YEE TAI-TAI (V.O.)

He's just performing for you ladies!

Back to the mahjong chamber. Close-up on Wang listening and laughing with the others.

The clatter of mahjong tiles.

LIAO TAI-TAI

Are we still going to East Asia for dinner tonight?
Aren't you tired of it?

YEE TAI-TAI

It's better to go there where we are protected by the
Secret Service.

WANG CHIA-CHIH/MAI TAI-TAI

It's that bad?

LEUNG TAI-TAI

Those crazy bombs! Things are really getting worse.
On the streets, they shoot anybody.

YEE TAI-TAI

(to Wang)

Hong Kong should be better, no? How are things over
there these days?

WANG CHIA-CHIH/MAI TAI-TAI

Always a scramble. Prices are up twenty percent. And
because of the war even the black market is drying up.

Yee Tai-tai offers cigarettes to Liao, and then to Wang.

YEE TAI-TAI

Oh wait, you don't smoke, if I recall.

WANG CHIA-CHIH/MAI TAI-TAI

(smiles)

In fact, I brought you some Marlboros. I left them in
my bag, I almost forgot!

YEE TAI-TAI

Aiyo! How can I thank you enough! We can't even get
them on the black market here!

INT. HALLWAY IN YEE'S RESIDENCE—SHANGHAI—NIGHT

Wang takes advantage of a break in the game to go upstairs.

CHANG (V.O.)

(exiting the study)

Minister, I understand.

Wang politely nods to Chang as she passes him in the hall.

Chang returns the courtesy. Wang walks upstairs, aware of Chang's gaze behind her.

INT. GUEST ROOM IN YEE'S RESIDENCE—SHANGHAI—NIGHT

Wang enters the room. Her unpacked luggage is stacked by the bed. She opens a suitcase and takes out a few packs of cigarettes.

She turns, and is startled to find Yee standing in the doorway.

YEE

The room is small, but at least it's safer than a hotel.

WANG CHIA-CHIH/MAI TAI-TAI

I didn't want to bother you or Yee Tai-tai—

YEE

She likes having a mahjong partner around the house, and I'm hardly home anyway.

166

WANG CHIA-CHIH/MAI TAI-TAI

Still so busy?

(looks him over)

You do seem to have lost quite a bit of weight!

Yee looks at her.

YEE

I find you somewhat changed also.

WANG CHIA-CHIH/MAI TAI-TAI

It's been three years, imagine, and the war is still not over. For us to be standing here, both alive, is already something. . . . I've brought a few things with me. The cigarettes are a gift for Yee Tai-tai. I'm afraid I don't really have a gift for you.

YEE

Your presence is itself a gift.

With a slight smile, he slips out the door.

EXT. SHANGHAI STREET—DAY

Wang descends from a tricycle taxi onto the crowded thoroughfare. She crosses the street and hops onto a passing tram.

INT./EXT. TRAM CAR—DAY

She sits down next to K'uang Yu-min. Discreetly, she hands him a piece of paper from her handbag.

WANG CHIA-CHIH/ MAI TAI-TAI

(in a low, fast voice)

Here's the floor plan. Back door is sealed, only outlet is the front entrance. Two drivers, Guo and Yao. Guo drives for Yee Tai-tai. Amah and the other servants are all from the same village as Yee. The drivers never leave their cars, probably double as informers. Everyone is searched before getting in or out of the car.

K'uang Yu-min glances at Wang.

WANG CHIA-CHIH/MAI TAI-TAI

Yee Tai-tai as always brings people home to play mahjong—wives of high officials. They seem to know a lot. A certain Ma Tai-tai—she's always watching me, I don't know why . . .

K'UANG YU-MIN

And Yee?

WANG CHIA-CHIH/MAI TAI-TAI

Saw him only once. He's mostly out or in his study. He's got a secretary, last name Chang.

K'UANG YU-MIN

What's his first name?

WANG CHIA-CHIH/MAI TAI-TAI

I don't know yet.

K'UANG YU-MIN

Be careful!

WANG CHIA-CHIH/MAI TAI-TAI

(pause)

I need money.

K'uang looks around, and at the same time passes her a magazine; hidden inside is an envelope containing money.

K'UANG YU-MIN

That's all for now.

(looks at Wang and smiles)

How come you play every day but never get better?

WANG CHIA-CHIH/MAI TAI-TAI

I can't concentrate.

Wang stuffs the magazine into her handbag.

WANG CHIA-CHIH/MAI TAI-TAI

How are they? Huang Lei and everyone?

K'UANG YU-MIN

They're fine. They're thinking of you. You'll see them again after all this.

INT. YEE'S RESIDENCE—DINING ROOM—SHANGHAI—
MORNING

Wang is having breakfast with Yee Tai-tai. A Ping-Tan ballad
from Soochow plays on the radio.

YEE TAI-TAI

Aiya, you should be glad you didn't go with me to the
opera last night. I came back with a headache!

Wang is reading the newspaper.

WANG CHIA-CHIH/MAI TAI-TAI

Which opera?

YEE TAI-TAI

Wu Jia Po! Aiya—it was out of tune and off beat, my
god! The top artists are all hiding out in Hong Kong.
So I told Old Yee, how could Wang Ching-wei's
government win the hearts and minds of the people if
they can't even bring a good show to town, right?

Yee enters, dressed to go out, a gentle smile on his face.

YEE

Good morning, ladies!

WANG CHIA-CHIH/MAI TAI-TAI

Good morning, Mr. Yee!

Yee sits down and sips his tea. He leans over and sees that Wang has circled some movie listings in the paper.

YEE TAI-TAI

(to Yee)

That turtle shell medicine shouldn't be taken with tea.

(to Mai Tai-tai)

His feet are always cold at night. I have to warm them.

Yee Tai-tai smiles and laughs a little.

YEE

(annoyed)

I have a meeting soon. Do you have plans for today?

YEE TAI-TAI

Liao Tai-tai wants me to play mahjong with her old mother.

YEE

(smiles)

I hope you'll not be forcing our guest along with you.

WANG CHIA-CHIH/MAI TAI-TAI

I've already been given leave. I am going to the movies this afternoon.

EXT. YEE'S RESIDENCE—SHANGHAI—DAY

A light drizzle fills the air as Wang walks under an umbrella, searching for a tricycle taxi, when a black sedan pulls up.

Yee's chauffeur gets out to open the door for her.

CHAUFFEUR
(in Shanghainese)

It's rainy. Master told me to give you a ride.

A little surprised, Wang gets into the car.

INT. YEE'S CAR—CONTINUOUS

Wang sits in the car, studying the streets.

WANG CHIA-CHIH/MAI TAI-TAI

This isn't the way to the Meichi Theater?

The driver says nothing.

EXT. APARTMENT HOUSE—SHANGHAI—DAY

The car turns into a quiet alley and stops by the back entrance of a small but expensive-looking apartment house.

The chauffeur opens the car door, an open umbrella in hand. Wang exits the car. He hands her an envelope. A squeeze and Wang can feel a key inside. The envelope is marked 2A.

The driver takes her handbag and trench coat, searches them, and hands them back to her.

CHAUFFEUR

The car will wait for you.

Wang looks around and enters the building.

INT. APARTMENT HOUSE—HALLWAY—SHANGHAI— CONTINUOUS

Wang takes the stairs and stops in front of apartment 2A.

She puts the key into the lock. It fits. The door opens.

INT. APARTMENT 2A—BEDROOM—SHANGHAI— CONTINUOUS

WANG CHIA-CHIH/MAI TAI-TAI

Anybody here?

There is no answer. Wang enters and closes the door behind her.

It smells musty inside the apartment—old velvet drapes, dust all over the place. A photo on the mantlepiece shows a white couple with two kids.

She walks into the bedroom. A window has been left open. It bangs in the wind, rain dripping down the wall beneath it.

She closes the window.

Sensing something, she turns around and gasps at the sight of Yee, sitting in an armchair, watching her.

WANG CHIA-CHIH/MAI TAI-TAI

Don't ever scare me like this again!

Yee just smiles. He lights a cigarette and takes a few puffs, watching her.

Finally, she walks to him, leans over, and, without taking her eyes from him, gently takes the cigarette from his mouth, dropping it to the floor. Yee stands up and grabs her head, trying to kiss her.

WANG CHIA-CHIH/MAI TAI-TAI

My hair!

YEE

Are you going to play hard to get?

WANG CHIA-CHIH/MAI TAI-TAI

Is that how you like it?

(pause)

Sit down.

Yee reluctantly sits down again.

Wang walks over to the window and, bending over, slowly begins to take off her stockings.

He watches her.

As she begins to unbutton her dress, he suddenly leaps up, grabs her, and pushes her against the wall, ripping the side seam of her chipao.

He flips her around facedown onto the bed, unbuckles his pants, and enters her from behind.

What follows is more or less a rape.

Her face opens, first in pain, then in an astonished, anguished mix of anger and pleasure.

Later:

The light outside is dying; the rain has ended.

Yee dressed, sits in a chair by the bed, on which Wang lies, curled up, quiet.

She turns and looks at him. He picks up her coat from the floor and places it on the bed.

YEE

Your coat.

He leaves.

She stares blankly, hardly seeming to notice. But then, an almost imperceptible smile creases her face.

INT. FANCY RESTAURANT—SHANGHAI—NIGHT

After a meal, the Tai-tais sit in a private room listening to a pair of Ping-Tan singers spinning their tales. On the floor are shopping bags from Sincere Emporium. In the hallway outside the room their bodyguards pace.

PING-TAN SINGERS

(singing)

They do not speak but secretly they wonder:
Why feelings go where feelings should not wander.
One is quiet with lowered head and racing heart
The other bows formally just to play his part.
She quivers with voice like honey.
He yearns with shattering folly
One says, Please—
The other says, Master—

The song continues throughout the following conversation.
Yee comes in to join them.

YEE TAI-TAI

Well, look who's here! Old Yee, how . . .

YEE

I'm hosting a party next door.

LEUNG TAI-TAI

Aiya, Mr. Yee caught us shopping!

MA TAI-TAI

What a rare honor. Stay and listen a bit!

YEE

Sure, just a little bit.

Wang barely registers Yee's presence.

Ma Tai-tai

You understand the singers' dialect?

Wang Chia-chih/Mai Tai-tai

A bit. I used to hear Ping-Tan all the time when I was a girl. . . . I miss it, you can't hear it in Hong Kong.

Ma Tai-tai

But now you're here.

Wang Chia-chih/Mai Tai-tai

Only for a while—I have to go back to Hong Kong soon. Please tell me what you need before I go. If I can make my way back, I'll make sure to bring whatever it is.

Yee overhears.

Int. Yee's Residence—Hallway—Shanghai—Morning

Wang walks down the hall alone. She checks the dining room—no sign of Yee. His hat is gone from the rack. Lost in thought, she's startled by Amah's voice.

Amah

Would madame want some breakfast?

WANG CHIA-CHIH/MAI TAI-TAI

No thank you, I'm not hungry yet. Where are Mr. and
Mrs. Yee?

AMAH

Madame Yee is still sleeping. Mr. Yee has gone to
Nanking on business.

WANG CHIA-CHIH/MAI TAI-TAI

To Nanking?

AMAH

Yes.

WANG CHIA-CHIH/MAI TAI-TAI

For how long?

AMAH

(suspicious)

I couldn't say.

INT. GUEST ROOM IN YEE'S RESIDENCE—SHANGHAI—DAY

Wang lies in bed, listening to the sounds of mahjong from
downstairs.

INT. YEE'S RESIDENCE—FRONT HALL—SHANGHAI—DAY

Yee Tai-tai talks to Amah before leaving.

YEE TAI-TAI

(in Shanghainese)

Liang Tai-tai tripped and hurt herself, so I'm going
over to see her. Mai Tai-tai still has her headache—give
her two aspirins when she wakes. And if she feels like
it, take some congee up for her.

INT. YEE'S RESIDENCE—GUEST ROOM—SHANGHAI—DAY

From her bedroom window, Wang steals a look at Yee
Tai-tai getting into her car. The car drives by the guards in
the alley.

Later:

Wang, nervous, sits at her dressing table, putting on lipstick—
then wipes it off. She pauses as she hears the gate open outside,
then footsteps coming up the stairs.

She bolts up, grabs a suitcase, and starts throwing her
belongings into it, pretending that she's packing.

The footsteps stop by her door. Wang takes a deep breath. The
door opens.

Yee stands in the doorway. Wang lifts her eyes to look at him,
without any sign of surprise.

Yee closes the door behind him and looks at her.

Wang goes and pulls shut the curtains.

WANG CHIA-CHIH/MAI TAI-TAI

What if I were to tell you that I hated you?

179

YEE

I would believe you.

Yee kisses Wang, fondling her breasts.

WANG CHIA-CHIH/MAI TAI-TAI

(murmurs)

I hate you!

YEE

I said I believed you. And you know, it would be the first time in a long time that I believed anyone, anyone at all. Let me hear it again, I want to believe . . .

WANG CHIA-CHIH/MAI TAI-TAI

You must be very lonely.

YEE

Perhaps, but I'm still alive . . .

WANG CHIA-CHIH/MAI TAI-TAI

You've been gone without a word for four days. I hated you every minute you were gone.

YEE

Do you still hate me, now that I'm back?

180

> WANG CHIA-CHIH/MAI TAI-TAI
>
> *(a beat)*

No.

> YEE

But you still want to go back to Hong Kong?

> WANG CHIA-CHIH/MAI TAI-TAI

Yes, I want to go back.

They kiss passionately.

Later:

Naked, on the bed, Yee on top of her—he takes her face in his hands, insisting that she look in his eyes.

Afterward, they hold each other.

> WANG CHIA-CHIH/MAI TAI-TAI
>
> *(whispers in his ear)*

You should get me an apartment.

INT. PEACE CINEMA—SHANGHAI—DAY

Wang walks into the dark cinema. Suddenly a hand pulls her aside.

It's K'uang. Squeezed into a small corner, they stand very close to each other.

WANG CHIA-CHIH

(talking fast)

I went to the teahouse to look for you . . .

K'UANG YU-MIN

Some of our top people were arrested. They raided a bunch of our safe houses. Ou-yang was in one—luckily he got away. We must cut all our connections. You are not to go to any of the old places.

WANG CHIA-CHIH

When are we going to strike?

K'UANG YU-MIN

As soon as they give the orders.

WANG CHIA-CHIH

(speaking almost robotically)

Tell them to please hurry up. And then we can all leave, right?

K'UANG YU-MIN

(concerned)

I can't say . . . I don't know.

WANG CHIA-CHIH

He's gone again. Amah said he went to Nanking, but who knows the truth? Maybe there's another woman. He took me to alley 1237 off Avenue Shi Fei the night before last . . .

K'UANG YU-MIN

We have it staked out.

WANG CHIA-CHIH

Perfume—jasmine—it was in the air. Not recent, though. There was dust on the pillows. I don't know, I don't know.

He touches her shoulder, awkwardly hesitates, his face close to hers, but then holds back.

K'UANG YU-MIN

Wang Chia-chih—look at me, look at me—

Wang Chia-chih takes a deep breath to calm herself.

K'UANG YU-MIN

You're going to be okay. I won't let you get hurt.

K'uang leaves, leaving Wang alone in the dark. The movie plays on.

183

MOVIE ACTRESS

Brother, you cannot break the law like this.

MOVIE ACTOR

I would never.

INT. YEE'S RESIDENCE—GUEST ROOM—SHANGHAI—NIGHT

Wang, lying awake in bed, tossing and turning.

She sees the hallway light in the crack under her door, and hears footsteps in the hallway. Then the figure on the other side of the door moves on, his footsteps falling away.

INT. YEE'S RESIDENCE—SHANGHAI—DAY

Mahjong playing, chatting.

YEE TAI-TAI

Yesterday Liao Tai-tai was bled dry!

LEUNG TAI-TAI

What happened?

YEE TAI-TAI

She was the sole winner two days straight, so she treated us all to a restaurant. And guess what, the minute we stepped into Shu-Yü, who did we bump into but Mr. Lee and his wife.

(guffaws)

As it turned out, Mr. Lee already had a full table. We added more chairs but still Liao Tai-tai had to sit behind me like a courtesan! She yelled at me to stop treating her like a piece of old tofu. I said old tofu makes the best Pock-faced Spicy Lady Tofu. Aiyo, we all died laughing!

LEUNG TAI-TAI

When she toasted Mr. Yee on his birthday it was like Pock-faced Lady Offering Longevity in person . . . by the way, where's Mr. Yee these days?

Wang listens halfheartedly to these old jokes. They reshuffle the tiles, with the usual clattering noises.

YEE TAI-TAI

He's gone to Nanking—again! . . . Let's be fair, she does carry her pockmarks well, unlike the wife of Chief Chien. Now her face is really disgusting—like a pancake dotted with black sesame seeds! No powder can conceal those! It drives me crazy. Oh, I win!

They all laugh.

LEUNG TAI-TAI

It's all because of you!

YEE TAI-TAI

Let me show you something.

Yee Tai-tai exits and then returns with a fur coat.

Yee Tai-tai

Look, it was fifty percent off!

Int. Yee's Residence—Guest Room—Shanghai—Night

Wang closes her eyes, and reopens them at the sound of a car stopping outside. The clock on the night table says four o'clock.

She listens as a door opens and shuts, footsteps, every familiar sound, all the way till another door closes.

Int. Yee's Residence—Shanghai—Night

Wang tiptoes barefoot downstairs to the second floor. She passes by the closed door of Yee Tai-tai's bedroom before going down the hallway. She notices a dim light from behind the study door.

She decides to take a risk. She opens the door.

Yee crouching down, burning pieces of paper in the trash can. He looks surprised. The shimmering firelight makes him look weary.

He gets up.

Yee

(quietly)

Close the door.

Wang Chia-chih/Mai Tai-tai

I've been waiting up for you.

YEE

Then you must be very tired. I am.

WANG CHIA-CHIH/MAI TAI-TAI

Yee Tai-tai said you were in Nanking again.

The fire dies down. Yee does not switch on the lights.

YEE

Don't believe everything you hear. I've just been busy.
We busted a Chungking secret cell. Got more than ten
Blue Shirts, alive. Highly trained agents. So I had to
interrogate them personally one by one.

Wang trembles slightly.

YEE

Ah, but I forget. You don't want to hear about my work,
do you? It's boring. You're so careful never to ask
about it.

WANG CHIA-CHIH/MAI TAI-TAI

It's your business. Just as you don't ask about my business. All I do is sit here, waiting for you. Maybe you are
seeing someone else. . . . I can't sleep. If this goes on
any longer, you too will slowly get tired of me.

YEE

So that's what you've been thinking these past days.

WANG CHIA-CHIH/MAI TAI-TAI

And losing money at mahjong! Losing all my hard-earned money as runner.

Wang's eyes glisten with tears.

WANG CHIA-CHIH/MAI TAI-TAI

(turns)

I better go back up.

YEE

Get some sleep. Let me take you someplace special tomorrow night.

He gives her a gentle kiss. She turns to go. As she reaches the door, she turns at the sound of his voice.

YEE

(soft but stern)

And don't ever come into this room again.

EXT. SUNRISE BOOKSTORE—SHANGHAI—DAY

Wang sits in a hired tricycle, slowly passing the bookstore. She leans back and takes a surreptitious look.

TRICYCLE DRIVER

Get out of my way!

The store is boarded up.

EXT. SECRET SERVICE BUILDING—SHANGHAI—NIGHT

It's dark. The sound of barking dogs. Cold and sinister.

INT. YEE'S CAR—OUTSIDE OF SECRET SERVICE BUILDING—SHANGHAI—CONTINUOUS

Wang sits in the back of the car, shivering. Her eyes scale the high barb-wired wall, to the building behind, where a few lights show through.

> WANG CHIA-CHIH/MAI TAI-TAI
> *(to the driver)*

Take me back.

> CHAUFFEUR

The minister said I was to have you wait here.

> WANG CHIA-CHIH/MAI TAI-TAI

It's been over two hours.

The chauffeur doesn't respond, lights himself a cigarette.

Two plainclothes cops exit through the gate, scanning the street. Chang comes out with Yee, who gives him some last instructions.

Yee is let into the car, clearly wound up, taut.

189

YEE

I had unexpected visitors.

(to the driver)

Let's go!

The car starts.

WANG CHIA-CHIH/MAI TAI-TAI

I'm freezing. You might have at least asked me inside!

YEE

(suddenly a restrained fury)

Inside there?! Are you serious? You'd like to make a
little visit to my office?

WANG CHIA-CHIH/MAI TAI-TAI

(scared)

Never mind. Let's just go.

He looks fiercely at her, studies her face.

WANG CHIA-CHIH/MAI TAI-TAI

Why are you looking at me like that?

YEE

(a pause)

You shouldn't be so beautiful.

190

Yee grabs Wang by the arm and pulls her toward him.

Wang Chia-chih/Mai Tai-tai

What are you doing?

Yee

I was thinking of you today. Chang, my assistant, complained. He'd come into my office, open his mouth, and sounds would come out, but I didn't hear a thing. I could smell you. It was distracting. Two men—we picked up this morning at the train station, Blue Shirts. One of them stabbed one of our agents when they came to arrest him, sliced his head half off, really. I went with Chang, to the chamber, to question them. One was dead already, his eyes broken. I stared at the other. I knew him long ago—we were classmates at the military academy. I couldn't talk to him, but I watched him. I started to imagine him, fucking you. The bastard. . . . His blood sprayed all over my shoes. I had to clean it off before I came out. Do you understand?

Int. Apartment—Bedroom—Shanghai—night

Wang and Yee in bed, having sex in the dark.

They roll over, Wang on top.

She straddles him, slowly moving.

She closes her eyes, slowly rocking on him, then opens them, looks at him.

On the chair next to the bed, his clothes hang. His gun and holster.

Her eyes drift to the gun, then back to him.

As she rides him harder, tears start to flow from her eyes.

EXT. AUTUMN—SHANGHAI—DAY

To establish: Circling doves over a working-class residential area in Shanghai.

INT. HOSTEL ROOM—SHANGHAI—DAY

Wang Chia-chih stands by the window of a room in a run-down old guest house, staring at the gray sky.

Old Wu sits behind her. K'uang stands by the door.

OLD WU

Did he really promise you an apartment?

WANG CHIA-CHIH

We'll see! He was there when I told Yee Tai-tai I was leaving next Sunday. He can't back out now, can he?

OLD WU

That's marvelous. That old wolf is really starting to let his guard down.

K'UANG YU-MIN

Once we have a precise location, we can start moving!

OLD WU

Not so fast.

K'UANG YU-MIN

What are we waiting for?

OLD WU

We need information, information! He broke a cell and stole an important shipment of arms sent by the Americans to us. That was a huge loss.

(mumbles to himself)

It's strange that the Japanese are also trying to locate the goods. I wonder if Mr. Yee would sell information to the Russians in exchange for his future. Wang Chia-chih is a precious lead which we must exploit to the fullest.

K'UANG YU-MIN

But she's not a trained spy. Look at her, she can't take the pressure.

OLD WU

You underestimate her. The best part about our Miss Wang here is that she carries herself every bit as Mai Tai-tai, and not an agent. She's come this far, that's no small feat. Our superiors are extremely impressed. The last two women I tried to snare him with were superbly trained, it's true, and they held his interest briefly, that's for sure. But he sniffed them out, and that was it for them. They even gave up the names of their entire cell.

K'UANG YU-MIN

You have no concern whatsoever for her safety?

(worked up)

She's done what she's supposed to do—get Yee hooked.
Now we should take over.

Suddenly, Old Wu drops his harmless demeanor and takes on a
truly menacing tone.

OLD WU

(slams the desk angrily)

Don't tell me what to do! Now you listen to me! Yee
murdered my wife, both my children! But I could still
eat dinner with him one table away. This is our work.
I'd like nothing better than to kill him, with my own
hands. But if he's more useful to us alive than dead, I
will let him live for a few more days.

(turning to Wang)

But you're going to keep him on the line, and report
every word he says until I give the order.

Dead silence. Wang's lip trembles.

OLD WU

As an agent there is only one thing, loyalty. Loyalty to
the party, to our leader, and to our country! Am I
making myself clear?

WANG CHIA-CHIH

Don't worry. I will do what you say!

OLD WU

(takes Wang by the shoulders)

Good! Keep him in your trap. And if you need anything . . .

WANG CHIA-CHIH

You think I have him in a trap? Between my legs, maybe? You think he can't smell the spy in me when he opens up my legs? Who do you think he is?

Old Wu listens, becoming increasingly nervous.

WANG CHIA-CHIH

He knows better than you how to act the part. He not only gets inside me, but he worms his way into my heart. I take him in like a slave. I play my part loyally, so I too can get inside him. And every time he hurts me until I bleed and scream before he comes, before he feels alive. In the dark only he knows it's all true.

OLD WU

Okay, stop it!

WANG CHIA-CHIH

That's why I can torture him until he can't take it any longer, and I will keep going until I can't go anymore.

OLD WU

(yells)

That's enough!

WANG CHIA-CHIH

Every time when he finally collapses on me, I think,
maybe this is it, maybe this is the moment you'll come,
and shoot him, right in the back of the head, and his
blood and brains will cover me!

OLD WU

Shut up!

She stares at him, almost defiantly.

Old Wu storms off. K'uang, almost in tears, looks at her, then
follows Old Wu out.

INT. IN THE CAR—SHANGHAI—FALL 1942—NIGHT

The chauffeur is driving. Wang sits in the back, alone.

Wang looks out the window. They've passed Wai Bai Du
Bridge, already beyond the old Western Concessions.

The car stops at a Japanese checkpoint. The driver shows the
Japanese guard his permit. The guard pokes his head in to
check.

Wang realizes that they've entered the Hongkou district, a
Japanese enclave.

WANG CHIA-CHIH

(uneasy)

We're going into the Japanese area? This was arranged by Mr. Yee?

The driver nods, and continues driving.

EXT. JAPANESE TAVERN IN HONGKOU—SHANGHAI— EVENING

Coming here is like going to Japan. The streets are thronged with Japanese. Bright colorful lights are everywhere. People walk around in kimonos.

INT. JAPANESE TAVERN—SHANGHAI—CONTINUOUS

Wang stoops to enter a small tavern. She can hear Japanese music, and people laughing and drinking. One glance at Wang and the hostess recognizes her, since she is the only Chinese there.

WAITER

(in Japanese)

Good evening.

HOSTESS

(in Japanese)

Welcome.

WANG CHIA-CHIH/MAI TAI-TAI

I'm looking for Mr. Yee.

HOSTESS

(in Japanese)

I know. This way please.

The hostess takes her to a room off the inner court, through a maze of corridors.

HOSTESS

(in Japanese)

Mai Tai-tai, this way please! Mr. Yee is waiting for you over here.

Private rooms along the way are occupied by Japanese officers and their geishas. Some of them have come straight from the front. They look dejected, listening to familiar songs from home sung by the geishas.

A drunken officer beckons her from his room, then rushes out at her.

OFFICER

(in Japanese)

Her! Come! Come in! Over here! Over here right now!

HOSTESS

(in Japanese)

So sorry! Colonel Sato, this is a customer, not one of our girls! Keiko-san! Keiko-san! Come and keep Colonel Sato company! Go get more sake!

The hostess restrains him. The man is unappeased, and storms back into the room in a fit. The hostess apologizes to Wang.

Hostess

I'm sorry.

Wang is shown into a room where Yee is already waiting with a smile. On the table are two small dishes of appetizers and a bottle of sake.

Hostess

Here is your guest.

She bows out of the room.

Yee

(pours himself some sake)

So . . . I punished myself, by making myself wait for you!

Wang Chia-chih/Mai Tai-tai

Why here?

Yee

I had business.

Yee is slightly drunk; the corners of his eyes look tired.

The shoji is not completely closed. Yee suddenly spots the Japanese commander Miura Taicho walk by with another man.

Yee lowers his eyes and pours himself some sake with his head lowered. Wang catches on, and gently closes the shoji.

Yee pours some sake for Wang. They clink their cups.

We faintly hear a geisha singing from a room down the hall.

YEE

You hear that? They sing like they're crying, like dogs howling for their lost masters!

(laughs)

These Japanese devils kill people like flies, yet deep down they're scared as hell. They know their days are numbered, since they got the Americans on their case. Yet they still hang around with their painted puppets, and keep singing their off-tune songs—just listen to them!

Wang listens in silence.

She snuggles up to him.

WANG CHIA-CHIH/MAI TAI-TAI

I know why you brought me here.

YEE

Why?

WANG CHIA-CHIH/MAI TAI-TAI

You want me to be your whore.

YEE

Whore?

(laughs)

It is I who was brought here. . . . So you see, I know better than you how to be a whore.

WANG CHIA-CHIH/MAI TAI-TAI

(tenderly)

Will you let me sing for you? I'm a much better singer than they!

YEE

Really? Hm.

Wang lowers her lashes and smiles. She takes a sip of sake, licks her lips, and stands up.

She positions herself in front of him, posing like a classic sing-song girl. At first her voice is barely a whisper, but then we can make out that she is singing "Girl Singing From Earth's End."

WANG CHIA-CHIH/MAI TAI-TAI

(singing)

From the end of the earth
To the farthest sea
I search and search
For my heart's companion
A young girl sings
While he plays his harp

201

> Your heart is my heart
> Looking north from my mountain nest
> My tears fall and fall
> Missing him she will not rest
> Ah! My man, even in hard times
> Love prevails.
> Who in this life does not prize youth as much as gold?
> A young girl to her man
> Is like thread to its needle.
> Ah! My beautiful man,
> We're like thread tied together,
> Never to be unwound.

As she sings, she closes her eyes, letting the sentiment take over. Her body moves with the tune.

Yee is at first amused, then attentive, and then he himself, as she finishes, closes his eyes, unaccountably moved, tears flowing.

Silence. He puts his hands together, applauds her, slowly at first, then faster and louder. She sits back down beside him.

He takes her in his arms. They kiss.

INT. YEE'S CAR—SHANGHAI—NIGHT

The car pulls over in the alley near Yee's house.

Yee and Wang in the backseat.

YEE

You go ahead. I have work.

WANG CHIA-CHIH/MAI TAI-TAI

At this hour?

YEE

(quietly)

Look. I want you to do something for me.

He takes an envelope out of his pocket.

YEE

Tomorrow. Take this to the address written on the envelope. Ask for a man by the name of Khalid Udeen Sandhu. You can remember that, yes?

WANG CHIA-CHIH/MAI TAI-TAI

Khalid Udeen Sandhu.

YEE

Yes. If he tells you anything, or gives you anything, you'll tell me, right? Just our secret.

Wang looks at him and nods.

She gets out of the car. It drives off.

INT. HOSTEL ROOM—SHANGHAI—DAY

A hand holds the letter over a small pot of boiling water. The flap curls and unseals.

Pull back:

K'uang and Old Wu. K'uang takes a small note card out of the envelope.

K'uang Yu-min

Yee's name. That's it.

Old Wu takes the piece of paper, holds it up to the light, studies it carefully.

Old Wu

(giving it to K'uang)

Put it back. What do you think?

K'uang Yu-min

I worry Wang Chia-chih may have been discovered. If we send anyone in to check it out first, we may be falling into their trap. But if she goes alone, it could be very dangerous. We should stay outside and keep watch.

Old Wu ignores him.

Old Wu

(to Wang)

You'll go, as soon as possible.

Old Wu looks silently at K'uang and then leaves.

K'uang stands speechless, then turns to Wang.

K'UANG YU-MIN

Wang Chia-chih, I'm sorry.

He hands her the letter, in a daze.

Wang Chia-chih walks downstairs. K'uang Yu-min follows her and tries to kiss her. She pushes him away.

WANG CHIA-CHIH

Three years ago you could have. Why didn't you?

K'UANG YU-MIN

You know why, you know the reason, don't you?

Wang leaves silently.

EXT. STREET—SHANGHAI—DAY

A taxi stops at a busy corner. Wang gets out.

She spots Ou-yang and another man in front of the Peace Cinema. Lai Hsiu-chin idles in front of the Madam Green House boutique.

Wang carries her handbag with the envelope inside. She checks the address—a jewelry store.

Cautiously she pushes the door and enters.

INT. JEWELRY STORE—SHANGHAI—DAY

She opens the door and enters a small jewelry showroom.

205

This shop is brightly lit inside, the walls bare like the inside of an igloo. A low glass case at the back displays birthstone charms: yellow quartz and some semiprecious pieces.

An Indian Shopkeeper in a Western suit comes forward.

The following scene is all in English.

SHOPKEEPER

May I help you?

Wang freezes momentarily, then speaks.

WANG CHIA-CHIH/MAI TAI-TAI

I'm here to see Mr. Khalid Udeen Sandhu.

The man pauses, looks her over.

SHOPKEEPER

Do you have something for him?

WANG CHIA-CHIH/MAI TAI-TAI

Oh yes.

She takes out the envelope to show him. Then hesitates.

WANG CHIA-CHIH/MAI TAI-TAI

I'd prefer to give it to him personally.

He glances at the envelope, smiles, and nods.

SHOPKEEPER

Of course. Follow me.

(to customers)

Excuse us.

He leads her to the back of the store, then up a narrow flight of stairs, at the top of which is a closed door.

He opens the door and speaks to the manager in Hindi.

SHOPKEEPER

She asked for you, by name.

MANAGER

(to Wang)

He says you want to see me? Please come, sit down.

Wang walks over. He stands and offers her a chair in front of his desk.

She gives him the envelope.

He opens it in front of her, sees the card, smiles.

He turns to open the safe. Wang looks around.

He comes back and sits down.

MANAGER

(to Wang)

Your friend, he said you were quite particular. In fact he was afraid to make the choice himself. So you can choose any one of these—and not to worry, the gentleman has taken care of the fee.

He opens a small jewel case. It is full of diamonds. Wang is stunned by the sparkle of so many diamonds against the black velvet lining.

MANAGER

I haven't set any of them yet. So you are free to decide the setting. It won't take long—I'll need to size your finger please, so that we can set everything, correctly.

Wang stares at the diamonds, speechless.

MANAGER

(smiling)

Yes? All right? If they are not good enough, we have more. I have something really unusual for you.

He takes out a second box from the safe.

Wang leans over as the manager opens ceremoniously each little compartment, until he reaches the last one and reveals a blazing "hot oil" pink diamond. Her face flushed, her eyes stay riveted on the sparkling pink stone.

MANAGER

Six carats.

WANG CHIA-CHIH/MAI TAI-TAI

Pigeon egg.

MANAGER

(leaning toward her to measure)

I know you will be a perfect size six.

INT. SUNRISE BOOKSTORE—SHANGHAI—DAY

Close-up: A telephone rings four times. A hand hovers above the phone, but does not pick it up.

A pause, it rings again. The hand picks it up.

We're in the stockroom in the back of a crammed bookstore—piles of books everywhere. K'uang Yu-min is on the phone, listening. Finally, he speaks in Cantonese.

Intercut:

K'UANG YU-MIN

Hello?

WANG CHIA-CHIH/MAI TAI-TAI (O.S.)

Hi! Second Brother! It's me! I'm calling from Kiessling Café. Everything okay at home?

K'UANG YU-MIN

It's fine.

WANG CHIA-CHIH/MAI TAI-TAI (O.S.)

I'm fine!—Just too busy to call. I plan to pick up that package today. Yes, it's all set—for now!

K'UANG YU-MIN

I understand.

Everyone in the room is listening intently.

WANG CHIA-CHIH/MAI TAI-TAI (O.S.)

Anything—else?

INT. KIESSLING CAFÉ—SHANGHAI—WINTER 1942—DAY

We're back with Wang in the café where we left her at the beginning of the film.

K'UANG YU-MIN (O.S.)

No . . . nothing.

WANG CHIA-CHIH

I guess I'd better leave now. . . . All right. See you later.

Wang hangs up the phone. She walks over to her table and sits back down. She drinks her coffee, takes a bottle of perfume from her purse, dips in a glass rod, and puts a few drops behind her ears.

She sees Yee's car through the window, picks up her coat and bag, slips them over one arm, and leaves.

EXT. KIESSLING CAFÉ—SHANGHAI—WINTER 1942

Wang comes out of Kiessling Café.

The chauffeur steps out to open the car door for her.

INT. CAR—SHANGHAI—WINTER 1942—DAY

Yee makes room for her.

YEE

I'm late.

(to the driver)

Route Ferguson, please.

Wang touches his hand and speaks to him softly.

WANG CHIA-CHIH/MAI TAI-TAI

Let's go to the jewelry shop first. My ring should be ready.

Yee smiles, nods, and leans forward to instruct the chauffeur.

YEE

Turn back.

The car turns back.

WANG CHIA-CHIH/MAI TAI-TAI

Hey, we missed it. It's that little shop.

The chauffeur parks and comes around to open the door.

EXT. NANKING ROAD—SHANGHAI—WINTER 1942—DAY

Wang gets out the car, jittery. The sound of Yee closing the door makes her jump.

She knows Yee is behind her. He catches up with her and puts an arm around her waist.

INT. JEWELRY SHOP—SHANGHAI—WINTER 1942—DAY

Wang feels a moment of relief once inside the shop.

YEE

(looking at her)

Are you all right?

WANG CHIA-CHIH

I'm fine!

The shopkeeper comes out, sees them, recognizes her.

SHOPKEEPER

(in English)

Ah, Miss!

The moment she lifts her head, she sees two men choosing rings at the counter. She wonders if they are part of the group.

WANG CHIA-CHIH/MAI TAI-TAI

(in English)

I was wondering if the ring was ready.

SHOPKEEPER

(in English)

I'm sure it is. Please follow me.

While he speaks, she watches from the reflection in the glass the two men choosing rings.

Yee also notices and turns around to look.

Again, the narrow stairs.

They enter the upstairs room.

The manager nods in greeting, rises from his desk, and bows.

MANAGER
(in English)

Welcome! Welcome! Please sit.

The manager bends down to open the small safe covered with green felt. He returns with a small box.

MANAGER
(in English)

The masterpiece is ready!

He gives the box to Wang, who opens it—a magnificent ring. She examines it, then slips it on her ring finger. It fits perfectly.

WANG CHIA-CHIH/MAI TAI-TAI

Do you like the diamond I chose?

YEE

The diamond in itself is of no interest to me—I just want to see it on your hand.

She looks at the ring's pink diamond, moving her hand this way and that to get a better look. Against her rose red nail polish, the pink on the diamond is quite pale.

MANAGER

Congratulations!

YEE

(with satisfaction)

Fine.

He takes her hand and looks at the ring.

With the manager watching them, they are more keenly aware of their being alone under the lamp, so close, yet so restrained.

With a smile Wang begins to remove the ring.

YEE

Keep it on.

WANG CHIA-CHIH/MAI TAI-TAI

I wouldn't want to wear it on the street.

YEE

Please. You're with me.

She puts it back on.

With his profile outlined against the soft lamplight, he looks, to her, tender and vulnerable—a man in love.

At this moment Yee and Wang both hear a car backfire. She winces.

Without thinking, she tells him softly:

> WANG CHIA-CHIH/MAI TAI-TAI
>
> Go, now!

He looks blankly at her, confused.

> YEE
>
> What?

> WANG CHIA-CHIH/MAI TAI-TAI
>
> *(a harsh, panicked whisper)*
>
> Go, now!

With one last look in her eyes, in a flash, he understands.

He jumps up and runs for the door, catches the door frame, and flies down the stairs.

EXT. JEWELRY SHOP—SHANGHAI—WINTER 1942—DAY

A flurry of footsteps run across the linoleum floor. The shop-keeper follows closely but does not block him. He rushes out the door while the shopkeeper stays to watch.

YEE

(yells at chauffeur)

Door!

The chauffeur, alert, quickly opens the door. Yee ducks in and lies flat across the backseat.

The car speeds away.

INT. JEWELRY SHOP—SHANGHAI—WINTER 1942—DAY

Wang hears the screech of the tires.

Pang! A door closes, or is it a gunshot?

She sits there, dazed.

The manager gets up and sees her out with a feigned smile.

She walks out of the shop wearing the diamond ring.

EXT. NANKING ROAD—SHANGHAI—WINTER 1942—DAY

A late afternoon bright winter light still fills the air as she walks out onto the street. Her watch says almost four-thirty.

On the streets, she looks around, but recognizes no one.

No tricycle cab in front, so she walks over to Seymour Road.

People throng the sidewalks and many tricycles zoom by, but none is vacant.

Walking past a dress shop, she looks at the wooden mannequins with their fur coats and pewter-colored tops with batwing sleeves and matching skirts.

She keeps walking, looking out for a vacant cab, or an unexpected attack from behind.

She looks across at the Peace Cinema. The crowd has left, no tricycle there either.

As she debates whether to cross the street to the empty cinema, she spots a tricycle cab coming in the opposite direction, a little red-green-white pinwheel tied on the crossbar.

WANG CHIA-CHIH/MAI TAI-TAI

Taxi!

The driver, a tall young man, sees her waving and quickly makes a U-turn and speeds toward her, the pinwheel spinning wildly.

Wang climbs into the car and pauses for breath.

DRIVER

Where to, Miss?

Not knowing where to go, she chooses a destination at random.

> WANG CHIA-CHIH

Route Ferguson!

> DRIVER

Going home?

> WANG CHIA-CHIH

Huh?

The sky begins to darken. Before they reach Ching-anTemple, she hears the whistles.

> DRIVER

Ah—they're blocking the road again!

A middle-aged man in Chinese-style tunic and trousers drags a long thick rope across the street, a whistle in his mouth.

From the opposite side another man holding the other end of the rope pulls it tight. The street is cordoned off.

Someone else rings a bell listlessly, no sign of urgency.

The driver rushes to the edge of the rope before screeching to a stop. He slaps at the pinwheel to set it going again.

> DRIVER

Can't go any further!

Wang watches the road. Cars and people are all grouped on one side of the rope.

She knows. She looks around for her companions.

No one in sight.

The driver turns and smiles at her.

DRIVER

Looks like a long wait!

MIDDLE-AGED WOMAN

Let me through! I'm late! I have to go home and cook!

POLICE

I could let you through for the doctor, but not to cook!

Wang sits back in the tricycle cab, her ears pierced by the shrill whistling. She feels the hem of her coat, the place where she sewed the cyanide tablet in.

INT. THEATER IN HONG KONG UNIVERSITY—1939 (FLASHBACK)—DAY

The group is up on the balcony. K'uang is calling her.

K'UANG YU-MIN

Wang Chia-chih.

Wang looks up at them from the empty stage.

LAI HSIU-CHIN

Come on up!

**INT. SECRET SERVICE HEADQUARTERS—SHANGHAI—
WINTER 1942—NIGHT**

Yee stands by the window, smoking.

Chang enters and places a file on his desk.

CHANG

We got six of them, all college students. They once ran
a drama group in Hong Kong. The woman is called
Wang Chia-chih, a student actor. The leader is called
K'uang—we've been tailing him for a while. A shame.
Almost got Old Wu, but he slipped out of town last
night. The gunman probably got away through the
back door of the Peace Cinema. When we searched,
they all had movie tickets on them, better to get away.
The students were only there as cover.

YEE

You've known about them? Why wasn't I told?

CHANG

(a sinister smile and a smarmy bow)

Well, sir—there was some question, given your
involvement with the girl. . . . In any case, all's clear
now! I have delayed her interrogation, assuming you'd
like to conduct it yourself?

YEE

She's downstairs?

CHANG

Yes, Lao Lou and Lao Fan have her.

We've already broken the others—they're a very easy lot. Their stories matched.

YEE

Then . . . I will . . . no. There's no need for further questioning, is there? I've—we've gotten what we need.

Chang hesitates.

CHANG

Certainly. Any further orders?

Yee looks at his watch.

YEE

Take them to the quarry.

Yee's voice is cold. He turns to light another cigarette.

YEE

Total news blackout. Dispose of them, by ten o'clock.

Chang understands—Yee is sparing her a torture session. Yee moves toward the door. Then Chang thinks something else.

CHANG

Oh!

He takes out the ring and places it on the desk.

CHANG

Your ring.

YEE

(pause)

It's not mine.

Chang goes, leaving the ring where he placed it.

INT. HALLWAY—SECRET SERVICE BUILDING—SHANGHAI—NIGHT

A cell door opens, and Wang walks into the hallway, her hands cuffed behind her back, escorted by two plainclothes agents. Her high heels sound particularly loud in the long dark corridor. She continues walking. The corridor is long. There's a spot of chalky white light shining at the other end.

EXT. BACK ENTRANCE—SECRET SERVICE BUILDING—SHANGHAI—NIGHT

Wang is escorted out.

She sees a military truck parked on the road. About eight soldiers with rifles mount the truck. Then she notices, with a start, K'uang Yu-min. Despite the distance, she can make out his bashed, swollen face. He lifts his head and sees Wang.

Her face freezes, her feet rooted to the ground. She now sees that the whole group is there.

SOLDIER

Move it!

The soldier gives her a shove. She walks toward the truck.

INT. YEE'S CAR—SHANGHAI—NIGHT

Yee, barely visible in the backseat. He searches his pockets for a cigarette.

The guard in the front seat takes a quick peek back at Yee, but does not offer him one.

Yee looks out the window.

EXT. QUARRY—OUTSIDE SHANGHAI—NIGHT

The place is huge and frightening, lit by starlight and the headlights on the trucks.

The open pit gapes like a ready grave. The sound of feet marching over loose stone.

The six are lined up on their knees, perched at the edge of the vast quarry. Two soldiers load and cock their guns.

Lai Hsiu-chin crumbles in tears.

Wang Chia-chih and K'uang Yu-min trade a final look in each other's eyes.

INT. YEE'S RESIDENCE—SHANGHAI—WINTER 1942—NIGHT

At the mahjong table, there are now three black capes facing each other. Liao Tai-tai has taken the place of Mai Tai-tai.

Amah opens the door. Yee enters the house.

LEUNG TAI-TAI (O.S.)

Why don't we go to Chiu-ju then. It's been a while.

YEE TAI-TAI (O.S.)

When Yang Tai-tai invited us last time, wasn't it at Chiu-ju's?

MA TAI-TAI (O.S.)

If it is not Szechuan, it's Hunan—always so spicy!

YEE TAI-TAI (O.S.)

If you can't take spicy food, you'll have no spice in your game!

Mr. Yee enters the mahjong room.

MA TAI-TAI

(smiling)

Ah! Mr. Yee is back.

Yee looks at everyone with suspicion.

YEE TAI-TAI

This Mai Tai-tai, what a piece of trash! Promised to invite us but is still not back.

Liao Tai-tai

Mr. Yee, the minute you left, Yee Tai-tai has been
winning and winning. She's inviting all of us
tomorrow. Will you join us?

Ma Tai-tai

(smiling)

Mr. Yee! Your wife is not like you—she doesn't go back
on her word! It's not easy to get you to invite!

Leung Tai-tai

You have to treat us, Mr. Yee, for we never manage to
invite you.

He only smiles.

The maid serves him tea. He glances at the thick curtains
against the wall. They cover the entire wall—how many assassins can hide behind? He panics, and suddenly walks over and
draws open the curtain.

Yee Tai-tai

Don't do that, it's full of dust! It's so late already—are
we still waiting for Mai Tai-tai?

Yee

I'm going upstairs to change.

MA TAI-TAI

Don't bother—we're going now. Unless you got dirty today or something?

YEE TAI-TAI

I should make an inspection!

The ladies continue with their fun.

Yee signals Yee Tai-tai to follow him and walks upstairs.

YEE

I'm going upstairs first.

INT. GUEST ROOM IN YEE'S RESIDENCE—SHANGHAI— NIGHT

Yee pushes open the door to Wang Chia-chih's room.

The room is in total darkness. He stares at her luggage by the wall.

Footsteps coming upstairs. Yee Tai-tai appears in the doorway.

YEE TAI-TAI

(whispering, nervous)

What's going on? Your assistant, that Chang, and two men from the ministry—they came by a couple of hours ago and took away some of her things.

YEE

(surprised, but calm)

Go downstairs. Say nothing! Say nothing at all! You understand? If anyone asks, just tell them Mai Tai-tai had an emergency and went back to Hong Kong.

YEE TAI-TAI

What happened?

Yee looks at his wife. A long pause. She begins to understand.

YEE

Just go down. I'll be there shortly.

Yee Tai-tai, fear creasing her face, walks away.

Yee sits there, in a daze.

Yee hears the women's voices, bantering, from below.

LEUNG TAI-TAI (O.S.)

Well? Who's treating us to dinner tonight, Mr. Yee or Yee Tai-tai?

MA TAI-TAI (O.S.)

Mr. Yee, of course! He promised! He looks so radiant tonight, it's only natural he should treat.

YEE TAI-TAI

All right, all right! Let him pay for our dinner at Lai-hsi restaurant. Let's go now!

                    MA TAI-TAI (O.S.)

The only things good there are the cold appetizers.

                    YEE TAI-TAI (O.S.)

It's true, German cuisine is good only for cold
appetizers. Let's have Szechuan then, for a change.

                    LIAO TAI-TAI (O.S.)

That means it's back to Shu-yü. Ma Tai-tai missed it
last time.

                    MA TAI-TAI

Shu-yü again? Aren't you tired of Shu-yü?

                    YEE TAI-TAI (O.S.)

You didn't have Leung Tai-tai with you when you went.
Leung Tai-tai is from Hunan, she knows how to order,
we don't.

The clock strikes ten.

Yee gets up, switches off the lamp, leaving only the hallway light
and the sounds of mahjong playing from the room below.

                    The End

ABOUT EILEEN CHANG (ZHANG AILING) AND TRANSLATING "LUST, CAUTION," THE STORY

Julia Lovell

"To be famous," the *twenty-four-year-old Eileen Chang* wrote, with disarmingly frank impatience in 1944, "I must hurry. If it comes too late, it will not bring me so much happiness. . . . Hurry, hurry, or it will be too late, too late!" She did not have long to wait. By 1945, less than two years after her fiction debut in a Shanghai magazine, a frenzy of creativity (one novel, six novellas, and eight short stories) and commercial success had established Chang as the star chronicler of 1940s Shanghai: of its brashly modern Westernized landscapes populated by men and women still clinging ambivalently to much older Chinese habits of thought. "The people of Shanghai," she considered, "have been distilled out of Chinese tradition by the pressures of modern life; they

are a deformed mix of old and new. Though the result may not be healthy, there is a curious wisdom to it."

Chang's own album of childhood memories was a casebook in conflict between the forces of tradition and modernity, from which she would draw extensively in her writing. The grandson of the nineteenth-century statesman Li Hung-chang—a high-ranking servant of China's last dynasty, the Ch'ing—her father was almost a cliché of decadent, late-imperial aristocracy: an opium-smoking, concubine-keeping, violently unpredictable patriarch who, when Eileen was eighteen, beat and imprisoned his daughter for six months after an alleged slight to her stepmother. Her mother, meanwhile, was very much the kind of Westernized "New Woman" that waves of cultural reform, since the start of the twentieth century, had been steadily bringing into existence: educated and independent enough to leave her husband and two children behind for several years while she traveled Europe—skiing in the Swiss Alps on bound feet. After Chang's parents (unsurprisingly) divorced when she was ten, the young Eileen grew up steeped in the strange, contradictory glamour of pre-Communist Shanghai: between the airy brightness of her mother's modern apartment and the languid, opium smoke–filled rooms of her father's house.

Yet while Chang's fiction was eagerly devoured

by the Shanghai readers for whom she wrote—the first edition of her 1944 collection of short stories sold out within four days—it drew carping criticism from literary contemporaries. For Eileen Chang wrote some way outside the intellectual mainstream of the middle decades of twentieth-century China. Although an early-twenty-first-century Western reader might not immediately notice it from much of her 1940s fiction—the body of work for which she is principally celebrated—she grew up and wrote in a period of intense political upheaval. In 1911, nine years before she was born, the Ch'ing dynasty was toppled by a revolutionary republican government. Within five years, this fledgling democracy collapsed into warlordism, and the 1920s through '40s were marked by increasingly violent struggles to control and reform China, culminating in the bloody Sino-Japanese War and civil conflict between the right-wing Nationalists and the Chinese Communist Party. Many prominent Chinese writers of these decades—Lu Hsün, Mao Tun, Ting Ling, and others—responded to this political uncertainty by turning radically leftward, hoping to rouse the country out of its state of crisis by bending their creative talents to ideologically prescribed ends.

Despite experiencing firsthand the national cataclysms of the 1940s—the Japanese assault on Hong Kong and occupation of north and east

China (including her native Shanghai) — Eileen Chang, by contrast, remained largely apolitical through these years. Although her disengaged stance was in part dictated by Japanese censorship in Shanghai, it was also infused with an innate skepticism of the often overblown revolutionary rhetoric that many of her fellow writers had adopted. In the fiction of her prolific twenties, war is no more than an incidental backdrop, helping to create exceptional situations and circumstances in which bittersweet affairs of the heart are played out. The bombardment of Hong Kong, in her novella *Love in a Fallen City*, serves only to push a cynical courting couple to finally commit to each other. In the short story "Sealed Off," two Shanghai strangers — a discontented married man and a lonely single woman — are drawn into conversation in the dreamlike lull that results while the Japanese police perform a random search on the tram in which they are traveling.

Defying critics who scorned her preoccupation with "love and marriage . . . leftovers from the old dynasty and petty bourgeois" and her failure to write in rousing messages of "youth, passion, fantasy, hope," Chang instead argued for the subtler aesthetics of the commonplace. Writing of "trivial things between men and women," of the thoughts and feelings of ordinary, imperfect people struggling through the day-to-day dislocations caused by war and modernization, she contended, offered a more acutely realistic portrait of the era's desolate transience than did patriotic demagoguery. "Though my characters are not heroes," she observed, "they are the ones who bear the burden of our age. . . . Although they are weak—these average people who lack the force of heroes—they sum up this age of ours better than any hero. . . . I don't like stark conflicts between good and evil . . . we should perhaps move beyond the notion that literary works should have 'main themes.'" Eileen Chang was one of the relatively few writers of her period who adhered to the belief, throughout her career, that the business of the fiction writer lay in sketching out plausibly complex, conflicted individuals—their confusions, frustrations, disappointments, and selfishness— rather than in attempting uplifting political advocacy. "This thing called reality," she meditated in a deadpan account of the bombing of Hong Kong, "is unsystematic, like seven or eight phonographs playing at the same time, each its own tune, forming a chaotic whole. . . . Neatly formulated visions of creation, whether political or philosophical, are bound to irritate."

Chang's lack of interest in politics and inevitable antipathy toward the strident aesthetics of socialist realism efficiently guaranteed her exclusion from the Maoist literary canon and impelled her to leave China itself. In 1952, three years after the Communist takeover, as the political pressures on her grew, she decided to abandon her beloved Shanghai, first for Hong Kong and then for the United States, where she lived and continued to write until her death in 1995. In the post-Mao literary thaw, even as Mainland publishers and readers delightedly rediscovered Chang's sophisticated tales of pre-1949 Shanghai and Hong Kong, critics were still unable to rid themselves of long-standing prejudice against her, belittling her work for its neglect of the "big issues" of twentieth-century China: Nation, Revolution, Progress, and so on.

Begun in the early 1950s, finally published in 1979, "Lust, Caution" in many ways reads like a long-considered riposte to the needling criticisms by the Mainland Chinese literary establishment that Chang endured throughout her career, to those who dismissed her as a banal boudoir realist. For while the story carries all the signature touches that marked Chang as a major talent in her early twenties—its attentiveness to the sights and sounds of 1940s Shanghai (clothes, interiors, streetscapes); its cattily omniscient narrator; its deluded, ruthless cast of characters—it adds an intriguingly new element to this familiar mix. In it, Chang created for the first time a heroine directly swept up in the radical, patriotic politics of the 1940s, charting her exploitation in the name of nationalism and her impulsive abandonment of the cause for an illusory love. "Lust, Caution" is one of Chang's most explicit, unsettling articulations of her views on the relationship between tidy political abstraction and irrational emotional reality—on the ultimate ascendancy of the latter over the former. Chia-chih's final, self-destructive, change of heart, and Mr. Yee's repayment of her gesture, give the story its arresting originality, transforming a polished espionage narrative into a disturbing meditation on psychological fragility, self-deception, and amoral sexual possession.

For until its last few pages, "Lust, Caution" functions happily enough as a tautly plotted, intensely atmospheric spy story. A handful of lines into its opening, Chang has intimated, with all the hard-boiled economy of the thriller writer, the harsh menace of the Yees' world: the glare of the lamp, the shadows around the mahjong table, the flash of diamond rings, the clacking of the tiles. Brief exchanges establish characters and relationships: the grasping Yee Tai-tai, the carping Ma Tai-tai, the obsequious black capes, the discreetly sinister Mr. Yee. Chia-chih's entanglement with her host is exposed with the slightest motion of a chin, her coconspirators introduced through a brief, cryptic telephone conversation, the plot's two-year backstory outlined in a few paragraphs. At times, the reader struggles to keep up with the speed of Chang's exposition, as characters and entanglements are mentioned then left swiftly behind: the disappointing K'uang Yu-min; the seedy Liang Jun-sheng; the bland Lai Hsiu-chin, Chia-chih's only other female coconspirator; the shadowy Chungking operative Wu.

The suspense reels us steadily along, through the wait in the café, the stage-managed visit to the jewelry store and the ascent to the office, and into the story's startling finale—the section to which Chang is said to have returned most often over almost three decades of rewriting. Chang draws us artfully into her heroine's delusion, enveloping Chia-chih's progression toward her error of judgment in the sweet, stupefying air of the dingy jeweler's office. Afterward we follow Chia-chih on her sleepwalk out of the store, sharing her surreal confidence that she will be able to escape quietly for a few days to her relative's house, until we wake at the shrill whistle of the blockade and the abrupt braking of the pedicab. Mr. Yee's return to the mahjong table brusquely exposes the true scale of Chia-chih's miscalculation: his ruthless, remorseless response, his warped sense of triumph. "Now that he had enjoyed the love of a beautiful woman, he could die happy—without regret. He could feel her shadow forever near him, comforting him. Even though she had hated him at the end, she had at least felt something. And now he possessed her utterly, primitively—as a hunter does his quarry, a tiger his kill. Alive, her body belonged to him; dead, she was his ghost."

This final free indirect meditation echoes with

Chang's ghostly sardonic laughter — mocking not only her weak, self-deceived heroine, but also her own gullible attachment to an emotionally unprincipled political animal. For Chang's obsessive reworking of Chia-chih's romantic misjudgment was, at least in part, autobiographically motivated. Like Chia-chih, Eileen Chang was a student in Hong Kong when the city fell to the Japanese in 1942, and she, too, subsequently made her way to occupied Shanghai. Also like Chia-chih, shortly after her return to Shanghai, she entered into a liaison with a member of the Wang Ching-wei government — with a philandering literatus by the name of Hu Lan-cheng, who served as Wang's Chief of Judiciary. In 1945, a year after the two of them entered into a common-law marriage, the Japanese surrender and collapse of the collaborationist regime forced Hu to go into hiding in the nearby city of Hangzhou. Two years later, having supported him financially through his exile, Chang painfully broke off relations with him on discovering his adultery.

Far beyond its specific autobiographical resonances, though, the story's skeptical disavowal of all transcendent values — patriotism, love, trust — more broadly expresses Chang's fascinatingly ambivalent view of human psychology: of the deluded generosity and egotism indigenous to affairs of the heart. In "Lust, Caution," the loud, public questions — war, revolution, national survival — that Chang had for decades been accused of sidelining are freely given center stage, then exposed as transient, alienating, and finally subordinate to the quiet, private themes of emotional loyalty, vanity, and betrayal.

A NOTE ON NAMES

There are two main systems for romanizing Chinese in English: Wade-Giles, developed at the end of the nineteenth century and widely used up until the 1970s, and pinyin, introduced by the People's Republic of China in 1979. Because of its subject matter and use of language, "Lust, Caution" is powerfully evocative of pre-Communist China, so the older system has been used throughout this translation, with the exception of the surname Yee (for which the Wade-Giles version, "I," might have distractingly confused readers) and a few of the place-names (Chungking, Tientsin, Nanking), for which the English transliterations most commonly used in the 1940s have been given, again in the interest of creating a period mood.

And here, finally, is a list of characters, in order of appearance in the text, to assist the reader in pronouncing and remembering the

Chinese names. Pronunciations are as written, unless otherwise specified in the parentheses following each name.

Wang Chia-chih (*Chia* pronounced as "jam" without the "m"; *chih* as the "ger" in "larger"): A student actress turned assassin's plant; Mr. Yee's seductress.

Mai Tai-tai: Wang Chia-chih's cover-name in the conspiracy — the Tai-tai (wife) of a fictional Hong Kong businessman, Mr. Mai.

Wang Ching-wei (*Ching* as "jing" in "jingle"; *wei* as "way"): A real historical figure, Wang formed a Chinese collaborationist government in Japanese-occupied Nanking between 1940 and 1944.

Yee Tai-tai (Ee Tie-tie): The wife of Mr. Yee, the Wang Ching-wei government minister targeted by the student plotters.

Ma Tai-tai: A member of Yee Tai-tai's regular mahjong circle.

Liao Tai-tai (Lee-ow Tie-tie): Another member of Yee Tai-tai's mahjong circle.

Mr. Lee: An acquaintance of the Yees in Shanghai.

Mr. Yee (Ee): The head of Wang Ching-wei's intelligence service and the target of the assassination plot; Wang Chia-chih's lover.

Chou Fo-hai (Joe Foe-hi): A real historical figure, Wang Ching-wei's second-in-command in the wartime collaborationist government.

K'uang Yu-min (Kwang You-mean): The leader of the student conspirators.

Liang Jun-sheng (Leeyang Rune-shung): Another student conspirator; briefly Wang Chia-chih's lover, forced on her by the circumstances of the plot.

Huang Lei (Hwang Lay): The wealthiest student conspirator.

Ou-yang Ling-wen (*Ou* as in "oh"; *wen* as "wan" in "rowan"): Another student conspirator.

Lai Hsiu-chin (Lie Show-jin): The only other female student involved in the plot.

Wu (Woo): A member of the anti-Japanese underground resistance in Shanghai, with connections to the Nationalist government in Chungking.

—*Julia Lovell*

PRODUCTION NOTES

Nanking West Road, Shanghai, 1942:
Built to Order

David Lee, Coproducer

Even before preproduction began on *Lust, Caution,* a great deal of attention was focused on the re-creation of Nanking West Road. Ang wanted a specific part of the Nanking West Road to be featured in the movie, and it had to look exactly the same as it had in 1942, when most of this story takes place. Many crucial moments in the film occur there.

To be able to cover those scenes, the entire area would have to be built. We needed a vast space where we could re-create a complete neighborhood to scale. Where would we find such a large space? How much would it take to re-create an area that mimicked central Shanghai in the 1940s? Could we afford it within the budget? Thus began what would be one of the biggest endeavors of the film.

The search for the property and financing started in late April. By mid-May 2006, we were in talks with a potential investor from Taiwan for this re-creation. At the same time Mr. Xue, the head of the Shanghai Media and Entertainment Group, wanted personally to invite Ang to attend the Shanghai International Film Festival. When he heard that Ang was unable to meet with him due to the fact that he was on a location scout for *Lust, Caution,* and some of the film was to be shot in Shanghai, he said, "Please let me know if there's anything I can do to help."

As Mr. Xue was not only in charge of the film festival, but was also the head of the corporation that owns the Shanghai Film Studio, Ang asked me to set up a phone call. Two days later, Ang and Mr. Xue discussed the possibility of building the Nanking West Road set on the Shanghai Film Studio lot.

The timing was right. Mr. Xue was very interested in the idea. The building of the Nanking West Road set on their lot would not only help the studio expand its facility, but they would also be able to rent out the set to other productions after *Lust, Caution* finished filming. With Ang's art department team involved in the designing of the set, it would turn out to be something never before seen. Since the studio was providing their compound, space was no longer an issue.

In mid-June 2006, Ang accepted the invitation to Shanghai International Film Festival. When he arrived in Shanghai, Ang and the production team were immediately taken from the airport to the studio lot to scout the location. Looking down from the top of the twelve-story tower in the middle of the studio, Ang and his art department team were able to map out ideas for the construction site. It could work—but it needed to be done in just four months!

Before Ang left the film festival, Mr. Xue gave him a farewell breakfast. During their conversation he told Ang, "Director Lee, the land is yours for the set. Money is not an issue. Just tell me, what is your budget? Tell me what you have and I'll take care of the rest. You need it in four months? Not a problem. I'll double, if necessary, I'll triple the construction workers. It will be ready in time for the shoot. What I really need from you is to get your art department here to guide the creation." Ang was very appreciative. It was a done deal. Mr. Xue's eagerness and determination for Ang to shoot the film at Shanghai Studios made it all possible.

Shanghai Studios now has one of the largest and most beautiful standing sets in the world, and there is talk of someday building hotels, restaurants, and tourist activities centered around it. And our low-budget film got the use of a huge part of a long-lost neighborhood of old Shanghai—all built to order.

"Mai Tai-tai, Pleased to Meet You!"

Roseanna Ng, First Assistant Director

In the initial search for a leading lady for *Lust, Caution*, the major headache for me was not in the casting itself, but in keeping it under wraps—much like the heroine Wang Chia-chih and her secret missions.

With many procedures yet to be approved and a media-targeted Oscar-winning director, every move had to be kept extremely confidential, even from the personal assistants.

Yet casting by nature is looking for the needle in a haystack. It was difficult to remain confidential when one had to publicly announce the search, post the ads, and carry out blanket screenings in schools, offices, and groups.

Our targets ranged from freshmen in acting schools to movie stars who already enjoyed some fame. It was natural for the applicants to want to know the name of the movie and of the director. For the screenplay, we could use something similar; but for the name of the director, our standard answer was: "An internationally renowned director, a big name."

Noticing that I was from Hong Kong, they would guess . . . Ng Yu Sum? Wong Kar Wai? . . . There was of course one more Chinese director known to all, the one who had just won the big award, but then no one would think that "he" would come back to China to film.

"I can't tell you, but it's a chance in a million. If you miss it, you'll be sorry for the rest of your life!" My earnestness must have impressed them, so they all came. According to orders from the highest authorities, Ang Lee's name could only be released once he was safely inside the plane.

Finally, as agreed, at a certain hour in the beginning of May, while the director was on his way to Beijing, the news was confirmed. We could now, thank heaven, mention him by name! But orders continued to arrive from the highest authorities: the director could be named, but the film would be referred to as "Prologue to *Crouching Tiger, Hidden Dragon*" for the time being. The secret mission continued!

When I met with Ang Lee for the first time, he described for me what he was looking for in Wang Chia-chih, our leading lady. That particular period, its special look and feel . . . with the parting instruction: "What others don't want, I'll take."

Odd though it may sound, I understood what he meant. His Wang Chia-chih would not be a cookie cutter of the current movie stars: no oval face, no big-eyed Barbie, no long-limbed willowy mannequin.

One day the auditions ran into some problems. We had to set up an ad hoc center in the Chinese garden of a training college in Beijing to continue our work. It began to drizzle, which threw us off a bit. Just then a girl appeared with her bike. Her hair was straight and black, and she had on a T-shirt, jeans, and sneakers, simple and plain as a student. She was completely unassuming, and her attitude let her blend easily into the sea of hundreds of other faces we had already auditioned. But still, we noticed her.

In talking with this plain girl and having her audition with the script, we witnessed a remarkable transformation. Almost instantly, she brought out a classic elegance rarely seen these days, as well as a certain impenetrable inner complexity.

A closer look yielded an angular face—wasn't she just the kind of delicate beauty described by the author Eileen Chang? . . . The girl's name was Tang Wei, and after months and months of searching, we felt like Old Wu must have felt when she came out from behind the curtain—we had met the "real" Mai Tai-tai!

The True Meaning of Difficulty

Doris Tse, Line Producer

One of Eileen Chang's well-known sayings was "Fame has to come early." Yet I happened to have met one whose fame came none too early—Ang Lee. From him I learned the true meaning of "difficulty."

Eileen Chang had described painstakingly in her story how her heroine Wang Chia-chih in the end paced up and down Nanking Road as she prepared herself psychologically for the eventual assassination of Mr. Yee. Nanking Road therefore took on a special significance. The director wanted a real street, not set fixtures; he wanted all buildings in their real-life proportions, and all building materials—concrete, brick, steel, wood—as close as possible to the original, down to the last door and shop sign. In short, the director demanded the highest possible degree of authenticity, with only four months to go before actual shooting would begin.

Since there were few photographs to go by, the art department had to rely on a lot of written descriptions, testimonies from historians, even oral recounting from descendants of former shop owners, before an authentic Nanking Road could be committed to paper. This part of the undertaking—research, design, and implementation—became a monumental expenditure in terms of human and material resources involving several departments. Once the street was up, we had to rack our brains to properly furnish some hundred-odd storefronts. Every shop sign and the merchandise on display had to be period perfect. Even fruits in a small stall had to be seasonally correct. Then there were the pedestrians milling about. Every one of them had to have a reason to be there at that particular moment; no one was just a casual extra. Every single detail went through endless sessions of meticulous plotting, review, and rereview before they finally all came together to become the real Nanking Road.

I remember the day I took Ang Lee to see the construction site in action. When he saw how between three hundred and four hundred people were working day and night to enable him to film on schedule, he turned and told me that he was truly touched. I was thinking: he created movies to touch his audience, while he in turn was touched by our contributions. Isn't this a great thing about moviemaking?

The "Killer Pizza Light"

Rodrigo Prieto, Director of Photography, ASC, AMC

During preproduction, Ang mentioned to me that he wanted to find a "killer light" for Mr. Yee to use in specific moments in the story. One such moment was when he and Wang Chia-chih are in his car driving from the infamous #76 Secret Service Building (his office) to an apartment he has set up for her. He tells her about his "job," which includes torturing suspects, and how he thinks of her sometimes while "working." I thought of creating a flickering amber glow in his eyes, which would be reminiscent of the glow of the red-hot embers used in the torture chamber to prepare metal pokers to burn the people being questioned.

To create this effect, I thought of many tiny bulbs flickering to reflect in his eyes, and decided that Christmas lights could do the trick. I asked Man Ching, my amazing gaffer, to buy strings of red, yellow, and white Christmas bulbs, and bunch them up on a two-foot-by-three-foot white card, which he did with the help of transparent plastic. The result looked very much like a glowing, flickering pizza, so it inevitably got that name.

We shot the interior car scene in a stage against green screen, and the exterior plates were shot weeks later by a second unit. I had electricians waving long poles with lightbulbs attached at the end of them on top of the car to mimic the effect of street-lights passing, and created fake "moonlight" for when the car was not passing a light. Each time one of the streetlights passed, we dimmed up the "Killer Pizza Light," as if somehow the exterior light bounced off something inside the car and reflected this amber flickering light on Mr. Yee's eyes. This way, we subtly created the effect of embers lighting him during his intense lines. I must say that the actual "Killer Pizza Light" looked quite cheerful and inoffensive if you looked at Man Ching's creation, but when it lit Tony Leung's eyes, it did add a touch of almost terrifying insanity to his gaze.

Eleven Days in Hell

Roseanna Ng, First Assistant Director

After *Crouching Tiger, Hidden Dragon,* Ang Lee was going for another action movie.

This time round we did not have Yuan He Ping as coach. There were no martial masters from different schools, no professional bodyguards, no deserts, no bamboo groves. All we had were one bed and two actors.

While plotting the scene, the director had already made it clear that he wanted no stunts but actual actors throughout, that sets had to be ultraflexible to allow walls and ceilings to move about as required by the superroaming camera, and that all equipment—dolly, minijib, maxijib, power pod—the whole works would be deployed.

First, we took in all the available research by experts covering erotica galore: books, manuals, movies and pornos, classical and modern, Eastern and Western. We wanted to absorb it all and create our own style.

Actually, creating our own style was only in my own imagination. For the few pages of love scenes, since the very beginning, had been kept under lock and key as classified information of the highest order.

Throughout the filming, besides the director and the two actors, only three other people were admitted: the cameraman, his assistant, and the sound assistant. To stay alive, they had sworn eternal silence. I haven't had any contact with them for a while now, so I have no idea if they are dead or alive.

Three love scenes, a few lines in the script, a small room. Normally, plot as one might, sending the camera to the ceiling or flat on the floor, after a few days you'd conclude that there's just so much one can do.

Yet those three beds, once in the hands of Ang Lee, were filmed for eleven straight days, fourteen hours a day. In other words, the camera rolled in front of the two actors in bed for a hundred and fifty-four hours.

First scene: violent illicit love.

The costume designers had to waste yards and yards of materials in search of the perfectly tearable materials. During the actual shooting, scores of chipao (body-hugging traditional Chinese dress) and underwear were ripped apart violently. The walls, as is customary with action movies, were fully padded.

Second scene: guest room in Yee's residence.

According to the script, after Mrs. Yee has gone out, Mr. Yee suddenly returns home and finds a very agitated Wang Chia-chih in her room. Protesting and clamoring to leave, Wang finally yields to Yee's embrace and kisses, and then . . . and then, there was no more "and then."

Because from this scene on, even I was shut out.

After having finished the first scene, the director canceled all the fancy shots for scenes two and three to allow maximum concentration on the part of the actors. During the shooting, the number of people working within the studio was reduced to a minimum.

Every day, the director first prepped the actors privately before inviting the cameraman to discuss where the camera would go. The cameraman then related the approximate placements to me to arrange for lighting, using body doubles. When all this was done, I would flip out the red card used by referees to clear the studio of any remaining staff. Then I would have the site manager climb up the ten-meter-high lighting scaffolding to scan every corner of the studio. When all was clear, we would then close all the doors and windows of the studio. Within the entire complex, barring the site itself, only four of us were permitted to remain: the supervisor, the script holder, the sound recorder, and me.

So the thousand-square-meter studio with its lonely three little rooms was inhabited by fewer than ten people, on- or off-site. Such was the precedent set by *Lust, Caution* in the brand-new Shaw Studios, reputedly the biggest and the most advanced in all of Asia.

The love scenes in *Lust, Caution* portrayed not only lust, but the struggle between lust and passion, and between love and hate by extension. The exposition of the complex and convoluted nature of the relationship between Wang Chia-chih and Mr. Yee relied solely on these scenes. One could imagine the pressure on the director and the actors. Even Tony Leung, the seasoned actor who had been through it all, was close to collapse when he emerged from the small room eleven days later.

I could not witness the filming, but could follow the sounds through the earphones given to me as usual by the sound recorder.

Even Ang Lee, the calm master mind behind all this, was sub-dued for quite a while after finishing these scenes.

Those eleven days, for the director, the actors, and those of us monitoring behind walls through earphones, were like days spent in hell. The moment the love scenes were declared okay, the supervisor, the script holder, and I rushed to the darkened site for a group photo to mark our deliverance.

"Pung!"

Sherrie Liu, Script Supervisor

After a few grueling days of shooting in the Hong Kong residence of the Yees, Ang told me that those days of work on
mahjong playing were merely practice for the REAL THING,
which was about to come up when we went on location in
Shanghai. And he was right. By the second week of our filming
in Shanghai in late November, when our Second Assistant Director, Ah-Long, and I began regrouping for prep work on what
became the infamous scene 2 (a scene that we had started way
back in Hong Kong in late August), I soon realized all of the
seemingly never-ending over-the-shoulder shots for the Hong
Kong mahjong scenes were nothing more than a tiny mound
compared to the colossal mountain of four glamorously attired
Tai-tais chatting up a storm about power and politics while playing a full-on mahjong game.

Ang had little knowledge on the insanely complicated tech-
nicalities of mahjong playing, so Ah-Long was delegated the
responsibility of supervising the game itself—instructing the
Tai-tais on exactly what tiles to throw out and to take in—and I
had the job of compiling a complete shot list for the scene based
on notes I had jotted down during a simulation rehearsal from
way back in late August when Ang tossed around ideas about
how he envisioned the scene cinematically. As the scene was a
few pages long—and riddled with insinuations in dialogue that

required reading between the lines by all of the Tai-tais, which therefore meant extra brain work for the ladies on top of their mahjong playing—Ang suggested we break up the scene into two parts when filming, which was exactly what we ended up doing. The real challenge for me then, other than the usual difficulties my job would entail in a scene like this, was to come up with a list of shots for Ang, our cinematographer Rodrigo, and the Assistant Directors that was both comprehensive and cinematically interesting. Scene 2 was not only an eye-opening mahjong scene in a movie that shows off four gorgeous Tai-tais in 1940s Shanghai, it was also part of the opening sequence of the movie that introduced our protagonists Wang Chia-chih and Yee Tai-tai for the first time. Along with the challenge came tremendous pressure. Ang's request had been to have shots from all three levels: the eye level, the midbody level, and the level of the mahjong table, plus a few special numbers linking the mahjong moves to certain dramatic moments. As a result, we started out by painstakingly canning away most of the eye-level shots first: both the POVs and the over-the-shoulders, covering all four sides of the table, and in most cases over both shoulders of the ladies onto whomever certain lines or looks were aimed. After that—more than a few shooting days later—we moved on to the more complicated shots that required dolly tracks, maxi jibs, knocking down set walls and whatnot. Mind you, this was all only for the first half of the scene, before the real dramatic moments were even approached.

All in all, the mahjong scenes of *Lust, Caution*—and scene 2 in particular—have proved to be more than just a new challenge for me. About a week after we had finished filming them, we were told to reshoot a few shots of Joan Chen (Yee Tai-tai) because it was feared that some of the negative might have been lost during transport. Right as we were setting up the first shot of the reshoot I felt a familiar achy sensation creeping up my spine. I mentioned this to Ang and he said, "It's the memories stored in your body about the mahjong scenes." The experience was that intense. I remember one day Drew, our production sound mixer, asked me, after many days of filming the scene, what the next shot would be. When I answered it was going to be a shot on Joan over Tony's shoulder, Drew, in all bafflement, looked me in the eye and asked, "How many shoulders does he have?" To this day I am amazed by how we were able to keep track of it all.

The Last Golden Light of Sunset

Rodrigo Prieto, Director of Photography, ASC, AMC

Every script I read has one or two scenes that are specially challenging for a cinematographer, and you usually know it as soon as you read it. In the case of *Lust, Caution,* however, I did not see it coming until Ang explained to me exactly what he wanted for all the scenes on Nanking Road after Wang Chia-chih takes Mr. Yee to the jewelry shop to pick up her ring. The script describes fading daylight, but Ang had something much more specific in mind. The set, built on the lot of Shanghai Studios especially for our film, is a replica of the intersection of Nanking Road and ShenSi North Road where Kiessling Café is situated. It was built to exact scale, with no forced perspective, so the dimensions were staggering.

Ang was looking for a color of light that you can sometimes see at dusk when the clouds in the sky reflect the last rays of sunlight, bathing everything with a pink-lavender color, similar to the color of the ring Mr. Yee has chosen for Wang. He wanted to use this color in the lighting on specific moments in the film, such as the scenes after she sees the ring at the jewelry shop. The idea was to combine rays of the last golden light of sunset with the ambient magenta skylight. The problem was that I had to maintain this light—that in reality lasts maybe ten minutes—throughout two weeks of shooting, all day long, on the Nanking Road set!

The main difficulty is that ambient daylight is very bright during most of the day, and it seemed impossible to create convincing sunset light across such a wide intersection since you have to overpower the daylight with electrical lighting. I was terrified of this scene as I did not know of any lights powerful enough to achieve this effect, especially given our limited budget. After researching the options, it seemed that the only lights that fit our requirements were some big units that were developed in Italy that bunch together many aircraft landing lights and are named after airplanes, like "Jumbo" or "Concorde." I thought we could not afford these lights. But, as it turned out, the company that carries them offered to let us use them for free! They arrived one day before we started shooting those scenes, which had me quite nervous, as I wasn't totally sure how bright they would actually be. We ended up using all of these lights plus many others we had already procured in Shanghai, all bundled together and focused down the intersection. This gave me barely enough exposure to look like the sunset light when the real sun was behind the buildings of the set; as the day got darker in the late afternoon, we had to adjust the lights after each take to maintain the same relationship between the artificial sun and the ambient daylight. This became quite stressful, as I had to keep measuring the exposure of the daylight vs. the lighting, and yelling at the crew to turn off bulbs or put nets in front of the lights every few minutes.

As for the pink/lavender fill light, it will be achieved in color correction at the lab, since it was obviously impossible to put colored gels on the clouds in the sky on top of our set. Figuring all this out and executing the plan took careful scheduling and many headaches, but I hope in the end it is worth it.

Not Your Standard Language-Learning Course

Drew Kunin, Production Sound Mixer

Mixing the production sound on any film presents a series of potentially difficult situations and puzzles to solve, but trying to do so in a language that is not your own can pose even greater challenges.

Lust, Caution is in Mandarin Chinese (or "Putonghua," as it's called in Mandarin), and has considerably more dialogue than an average film. This is the sixth time I've done the production recording and mixing on a film for Ang Lee, and although I was with him in China on *Crouching Tiger, Hidden Dragon,* I found this film to be much more difficult. Admittedly we didn't have the extremely remote locations and lack of infrastructure and accommodations that made that earlier film such an adventure (and logistical headache), but from a production sound mixing perspective this film was definitely more complex. My many months in China on *Crouching Tiger* familiarized me with the Chinese language, and I had learned to say simple sentences, but long scenes of intricate and fast-moving dialogue with multiple characters was beyond my level of comprehension.

Luckily there is a secondary form of writing, used primarily in the People's Republic as a tool for teaching children to write Chinese. This is called "pinyin," and it is a system using the Latin alphabet (the same as we use for English) to phonetically spell out Chinese words in transliteration.

Each day of shooting, as part of my preparation, I would make an elaborate guide to the day's dialogue. Working with my sound crew (Malau from Taiwan, Jessie from Hong Kong, and Da Ge from Shanghai) as well as with Sherrie, our script supervisor, I would handwrite pages of pinyin translation, then code each line of dialogue with multicolored highlighter pens, depending on which character was speaking. Blue for Mr. Yee, for example, or red for Wang Chia-chih. I would then tape these sheets together vertically so that I wouldn't have to turn pages while mixing the tracks. On some of the longer scenes with many characters (such as the mahjong scenes) I would have sheets several feet long draped scroll-like from rigging on my sound cart; these were covered with a rainbow of colored stripes that helped me to follow along and guided me through the scene.

As Ang rehearsed each scene with the actors, and then later, as we began to shoot them and the additional angles of coverage, I intuitively felt the scene and the lines better, and had less need to rely on my colored cue sheets. Nonetheless, they were an indispensable tool that helped me become immersed in every scene and allowed me to mix the sound without being obstructed by the language barrier.

As an added bonus, my Chinese language skills improved considerably. It may not be your standard language-learning course, but it was quite effective for me.

"Go, Now!"

Tim Squyres, Editor, A.C.E.

The scene in which Wang and Mr. Yee visit the jewelry shop together is the kind of scene that makes editors nervous when they read a script. Wang makes a decision contrary to what she has been leading up to throughout the entire film. There's very little that one can do editorially to help explain it; making Wang's decision understandable was going to be almost entirely up to the actors, who were given no lines to help them.

Understanding a character's motivation in a scene depends not just on what they say and do in that scene but also on the context in which that scene takes place, and the scenes that precede this scene are where Ang went to help make the jewelry store scene work. The intensity of the intimate scenes between Yee and Wang was much greater than I had expected, which helped to raise the emotional stakes for Wang. Also, the scene in which Wang breaks down when talking to K'uang and Wu gives Wang the chance to explain her state of mind, and the depth of her emotional entanglement with Yee.

The actors do a superb job with the scene. Wang is overwhelmed with emotion, but there's no real name for what that emotion is. Anguished confusion, maybe. This is not a simple thing for an actor to convey, but Tang Wei embodies it perfectly. I was worried about what she would do in this scene for months, but when I saw the footage I felt what she was feeling immediately. In the story we realize that the thing that derails Wang's plans is the feeling, at this moment, that Yee loves her. Tony Leung was given the extraordinarily difficult job of portraying this without being able to say it, and the simplicity and effectiveness of his performance is amazing. My job was simply to keep the focus of the scene on their emotions, and to not get in the way by overcutting. Once Wang touches the ring, the jeweler remains an offscreen voice, and we focus entirely on Wang and Yee. Once the dialogue stops and Yee looks at the ring on Wang's finger, we cut to Yee only when Wang actually looks at him, while we cut to Wang without regard to Yee's attention. The effect, hopefully, is to make the viewer's psychological identification entirely with Wang, that is, to make the shots of Yee feel like Wang's point of view, while those of Wang become the viewer's point of view. The moment of realization we see on Yee's face is chilling, and the very brief flurry of action that follows hopefully feels like punctuation, rather than like any real change in tone.

FILM CREDITS

美國焦點影業　　河流道娛樂事業

海上影業有限公司

出品

Focus Features and River Road Entertainment present
in association with
Haishang Films

銀都機構有限公司　　上海影視集團

聯合出品

and
Sil-Metropole Organisation Ltd
and Shanghai Film Group

色 | 戒

Lust, Caution

導演　　　李安

Directed by　　Ang Lee

劇本　　　王蕙玲　　詹姆斯·夏慕斯

Screenplay by　Wang Hui Ling　and　James Schamus

"色，戒" 原著短篇小說　　　張愛玲

Based on the short story "Se, Jei" by　　Eileen Chang

監製　　　江志強　　李安　　詹姆斯·夏慕斯

Produced by　　Bill Kong　　Ang Lee　　James Schamus

執行監製　　　宋岱　　任仲倫　　邵在純

| Executive Producers | Song Dai | Ren Zhong Lun | Darren Shaw |

聯合執行監製　　　王蕙玲　　林炳坤

Co-executive Producers　　Wang Hui Ling　　Stephen Lam

271

聯合監製　　　謝家慧　　　李良山

Co-Producers　　　Doris Tse　　　David Lee

攝影指導　　　羅德里格 · 皮耶沱

Director of Photography　　　Rodrigo Prieto, ASC, AMC

剪接　　　提姆 · 史奎雅斯

Editor　　　Tim Squyres, ACE

藝術指導　　　朴若木

Production Designer　　　Pan Lai

作曲　　　亞歷山大 · 迪斯皮拉特

Music by　　　Alexandre Desplat

梁朝偉

Tony Leung Chiu Wai

湯唯

Tang Wei

陳沖

Joan Chen

王力宏

Wang Leehom

演員表

易先生	梁朝偉
王佳之 / 麥太太	湯唯
易太太	陳沖
鄺裕民	王力宏
老吳	庹宗華
賴秀金	朱芷瑩
黃磊	高英軒
梁潤生	柯宇綸
歐陽靈文 / 麥先生	阮德鏘
曹副官	錢嘉樂
馬太太	蘇岩
蕭太太	何賽飛
佳芝舅媽	宋茹惠
張秘書	樊光耀

（特別客串）珠寶店經理	
（友情客串）舅媽牌友	盧燕
梁太太	劉潔
朱太太	余亞
廖太太	王琳
上海易家阿媽	華棟
日本酒館老闆娘	竹下明子
日本佐藤大佐	藤木勇人
日本酒館藝妓	瀬戶摩純
日本酒館樂師	小山典子
珠寶店印籍店員	

CAST

Mr. Yee	TONY LEUNG CHIU WAI
Wang Chia Chih / Mak Tai Tai	TANG WEI
Yee Tai Tai	JOAN CHEN
Kuang Yu Min	WANG LEEHOM
Old Wu	TOU CHUNG HUA
Lai Hsiu Chin	CHU JR YING
Huang Lei	KAO YING HSUAN
Liang Jun Sheng	KO YU LIEN
Ouyang Ling Wen / Mr. Mak	JOHNSON YUEN
Tsao	CHIN KA LOK
Ma Tai Tai	SU YAN
Hsiao Tai Tai	HE SAI FEI
Wang's Aunt	SONG RU HUI
Secretary Chang	FAN KUANG YAO
Jewelry Shop Manager	ANUPAM KHER
Mahjong Partner of Aunt	LISA YEN LU
Leung Tai Tai	LIU JIE
Chu Tai Tai	YU YA
Liao Tai Tai	WANG LIN
Shanghai Yee's Amah	HUA DONG
Japanese Tavern Boss Lady	TAKESITA AKIKO
Japanese Colonel Sato	FUJKI HAYATO
Geisha in Japanese Tavern	SETO MASUMI
Musician in Japanese Tavern	KOYAMA NORIKO
Jewelry Shop Indian Shopkeeper	SHAYAM PATHAK

香港裁縫師傅	顧章平
評彈男藝人	高博文
評彈女藝人	郁群
易太太司機	宋建華
港大劇場觀眾甲	劉日東
港大劇場觀眾乙	黎玉清
日本三浦司令	小島祐二
日本女老師	溝上陽子
日本酒館女侍應	南方文香
新凱司令咖啡廳侍者	安尼斯
三輪車伕	唐亞俊
日本酒館服員	李新
在警戒線婦女	石洪
在警戒線警察	陳崗
飲花酒妓女	鄧維
賣書老人	李斗

選角	吳惠姍

工作人員

第一副導演	吳惠姍
第二副導演	林子雄
場記	劉怡君
台灣選角	李崗
	王耿瑜
	李秀鑾

Hong Kong Tailor	GU ZHANG-PING
Male Ping-tan Singer	GAO BO-WEN
Female Ping-tan Singer	YU QUN
Yee Tai Tai's Chauffeur	SONG JIAN HUA
HKU Theater Audience A	LAU YAT TUNG
HKU Theater Audience B	LAI YUK CHING
Japanese Commander Taicho	YUJI KOJIMA
Japanese Teacher	MIZOGOMI YOKO
Japanese Tavern Waitress	MINAMIKATA FUMIKA
New Kiessling Café Waiter	ANYS FATNASSI
Tricycle Cab Driver	TANG YA JUN
Japanese Tavern Waiter	LI XIN
Woman at Police Line	SHI HONG
Policeman at Police Line	CHEN GANG
Prostitute in Brothel	DENG WEI
Old Man at Bookstore	LI DOU
Casting by	ROSANNA NG

CREW

First Assistant Director	ROSANNA NG
Second Assistant Director	LAM TZE HUNG
Script Supervisor	SHERRIE LIU
Additional Casting—Taiwan	LEE KHAN
	ANGELIKA WANG
	LEE HSIU LUAN

製片	彭惠鶯
	李超華
助理監製（邵氏製片廠）	趙以仁
劇務	謝志華
	張育華
執行製片	莫美芬
	倪順才
	梁詩敏
	梁志安
	譚靜顏
執行美術總監	劉世運
美術指導	莊國榮
	莫少宗
	雷楚雄
	林子喬
助理美術	李清渝
	莊曉媚
	李健威
	馮淑芬
攝影大助	林炳華
攝影二助	陳堯亮
B 機攝影	黃岳泰
	蔡崇輝

278

Production Managers	PANG WAI LUEN
	LEE CHIU WAH
Associate Producer (Shaw Studios)	LLOYD CHAO
Unit Managers	TSE CHI WAH
	CHEUNG YUK WAH
Assistant Production Managers	MOK MEI FUN
	NGAI SHUN CHOI
	YINDY LEUNG
	LEUNG CHI ON
	CONNIE TAM
Supervising Art Director	OLYMPIC LAU SAI WAN
Art Directors	JOEL CHONG
	ALEX MOK
	BILL LUI
	ERIC LAM
Assistant Art Directors	FION LI
	OLIVIA CHONG
	LEE KIN WAI
	CINNIE FUNG
A Camera Focus Puller	KENNY LAM
B Camera Focus Puller	EDMOND CHAN
B Camera Operators	ARTHUR WONG
	CHOI SHUN FAI

	林炳華
	錢翔
特技拍攝	林國華
	陳志英
劇照	陳錦泉
燈光師	伍文拯
推軌員	臧志良
燈光助理	羅榮堂
	范偉成
電工	梁偉雄
	吳明興
	文振榮
	伍文尊
助理推軌員	霍劍明
機工	劉年平
	鄺舜恩
	梁榮康
	蔡惠敏
化粧	關莉娜
髮型指導	李連娣
服裝指導	呂鳳姍
	歐陽霞
助理服裝指導	王寶儀

	KENNY LAM
	CHIEN HSIANG
SFX Camera Operators	ARDY LAM
	CHAN CHI YING
Still Photographer	CHAN KAM CHUEN
Gaffer	ANDY NG MAN CHING
Key Grip	LOUIS JONG CHI LEUNG
Best Boy Electricians	LAW WING TONG
	FAN WAI SHING
Electricians	LEUNG WAI HUNG
	NG MING HING
	MAN CHUN WING
	NG MAN CHUEN
Assistant Dolly Grip	FOK KIM MING
Grips	LAU LIN PING
	KWONG SUN YAN RAYMOND
	LEUNG WING HONG
	TSOI WAI MAN KUBBIE
Makeup	KWAN LEE NA
Hair Stylist	LIN TAI
Wardrobe Supervisors	LUI FUNG SHAN
	CONNIE AU YEUNG
Assistant Wardrobe	BOEY WONG

童堯

服裝管理　陸霞芳

道具領班　黃世傑
　　　　　賴伯勝
　　　　　程偉賢
道具助理　周敏
　　　　　梁英華
　　　　　張冠橋
　　　　　布偉棠
　　　　　朱德強
　　　　　陳俊廷

現場收音　老朱
收音持杆員　康永樫
收音助理　曾翠珊

總會計　謝玉貞
會計　胡麗蓮

語言指導　樊光耀
演員訓練　羅北安
　　　　　朱宏章
麻將指導　李嘉茜
湯唯儀態指導　潘迪華
舞蹈老師　屈網權

	MIRIAM
Wardrobe Assistant	LUK HA FONG
Prop Masters	WONG SAI KIT
	LAI PAK SHING
	CHING WAI YIN
Prop Assistants	CHOW MEN
	LEUNG YING WAH
	CHEUNG KOON KIU
	BO WAI TONG
	CHU TAK KEUNG
	CHAN CHUN TING
Special Effects	CHI SHUI TIM
Production Sound Mixer	DREW KUNIN
Boom Operator	KANG YUNG CHIEN
Sound Assistant	TSANG TSUI SHAN
Supervising Production Accountant	JOYCE HSIEH
Accountant	WINKY WU
Dialogue Coach	FAN KWONG YAO
Actor Training	LO PEI ON
	CHU HORNG CHANG
Mahjong Instructor	JESSIE LEE
Etiquette Training to Tang Wei	REBECCA POON
Dance Instructor	WALTER WAT

導演助理	周顯揚
監製助理	柯蒂亞·歐迪卡
聯合監製助理	黎淑韻
攝影師助理	容嘉樂
梁朝偉助理	黃蕙莛
王力宏助理	鄭俊豪
辦公室聯絡	陳淑雯
製片助理	吳凱恩
副導助理	卓翔
	劉永泰
花絮拍攝	洪光賢
	張子祥
劇本翻譯	廖端丽
	李巨源
研究	杜緻朗
"色,戒" 圖章設計	區大為
動作場面設計	錢嘉樂
動作場面設計助理	黃偉輝
打鬥替身	區榮顯
	梁博恩
	吳彰鵬
	黃凱森
	吳永倫

Assistant to Director	ROY CHOW
Assistant to James Schamus	CLAUDIA ODIAKA
Assistant to Co-producer	CANDY LAI
Assistant to D.P.	YUNG KA LOK, BILLY
Assistant to Tony Leung	IVY HUANG
Assistant to Wang Leehom	BRUCE CHENG
Production Office Coordinator	CHAN SHUK MAN JOANNE
Production Assistant	NG HOI YAN, HEIDI
AD Department Assistants	CHEUK CHEUNG
	LAU WING TAI
Making of	BRIAN HUNG
	CHEUNG TSZ CHEUNG
Script Translators	DIANA LIAO
	PETER LEE
Researcher	TO CHI LONG CHRISTINE
"Se, Jei" Chop Design	OU DA WEI
Stunt Coordinator	CHIN KA LOK
Assistant to Stunt Coordinator	WONG WAI FAI
Stunts	AU WING HIN
	LEUNG POK YAN
	WCH ANG PENG
	HUANG KAI SEN
	NG WING LUN

Film Credits

梁朝偉光替	洪展明
	李志健
	呂明明
	葉楠
湯唯光替	朱嘉茵
	趙羽君
	董艷
王力宏光替	黃健東
	張寶華

<u>上海工作人員</u>

製片主任	孫誕
	劉二東
	劉健華
協理製片	过強
聯合監製（上海影視集團）	許朋樂
	汪天云
	田鋒
策劃（上海影視集團）	傅文霞
外聯製片	陳風雷
	孟繁華
	赵俊杰
	刘志华
	華熔
现场製片	孫连宇
劇務	杜海

Stand Ins for Tony Leung	BEN HUNG
	LEE CHI KIN
	LU MING MING
	YE NAN
Stand Ins for Tang Wei	CHU KA YAN
	CINDY ZHOU
	DONG YAN
Stand In for Wang Leehom	DEREK WONG
	ZHANG BAO HUA

SHANGHAI UNIT

Production Managers	SUN DAN
	LIU ER DONG
	LIU JIAN HUA
Associate Production Manager	GUO QIANG
Co-Producers (Shanghai Film Group)	XU PENGLE
	WANG TIAN YUN
	TIAN FENG
Associate Producer (Shanghai Film Group)	FU WEN XIA
Location Managers	CHEN FENG LEI
	MENG FAN HUA
	ZHAO JUN JIE
	LIU ZHI HUA
	HUA RONG
Unit Production Manager	SUN LIAN YU
Production Assistants	DU HAI

生活製片　張百瑞
　　　　　吳佩東
　　　　　徐丹
　　　　　高興福
　　　　　程

现场第三副導　吴洁
上海演员副導　缪良
　　　　　　　唐亚俊
　　副導助理　周曦
　　　　　　　吴雷鳴
　大場面副導　张进战
　　　　　　　水磊
　　場記助理　江芹

　　助理美術　蓝斌
　　　　　　　于庆华
　　　　　　　赵娜莉
　　　　　　　姚俊
　　　　　　　曲继伟
　　　　　　　殷锦梁
　　　　　　　贤瑞清
　　　　採購　翁侃
　　　　　　　谢亮

　　摄影助理　杨德俊

	ZHANG BAI RUI
	WU PEI DONG
	LIU JUN
Production Office Coordinators	GAO XING
	CHENG FU
Assistant Production Manager	TSUI DAN
Third Assistant Director	WU JIE
AD Department—Extras Casting	MIAO LIANG
	TANG YA JUN
Casting Assistants	ZHOU XI
	WU LEI MING
Add'l Asst. Dir.—Crowds Scenes	ZHANG JIN ZHAN
AD Department Add'l Asst	SHIU LEI
Script Supervisor Assistant	REBECCA CHANG
Assistant Art Directors	LAN BIN
	YU QING HA
	ZHAO NA LI
	YAO JUN
	QU JI WEI
	YIN JIN LIANG
	XIAN RUI QING
Buyers	WENG KAN
	XIE LIANG
Camera Assistants	YANG DE JUN

謝義林

劉繼華

呂永偉

收音助理　陈远伍

助理服裝　奚彩芬

服裝助理　景春芳

陈明

赵汉

瞿红雷

助理化妆　陈溯源

李会艳

张洪双

助理髮型　任辉

蒋庆梅

王欣

置景領班　胡中权

道具領班　刘培德

道具助理　袁林根

张应鸣

王聖根

管建軍

槍械　卢根荣

徐康亮

	XIE YI LIN
	LIU JI HUA
	LU YONG WEI
Sound Assistant	ZHEN YUEN WU
Assist Wardrobe Supervisor	XI CAI FEN
Wardrobe Assistants	JING CHUN FANG
	CHEN MING
	ZHAO HAN
	QU HONG LEI
Assistant Make-up	CHEN SU YUAN
	LI HUI YAN
	ZHANG HONG SHUANG
Assistant Hair Stylist	REN HUI
	JIANG QING MEI
	WANG XIN
Set Decorator	HU ZHONG QUAN
Prop Master	LIU PEI DE
Prop Assistants	YUAN LIN GEN
	ZHANG YING MING
	WANG ZHENG GEN
	GUAN JIAN JUN
Firearms	LU GEN RONG
	XU KANG LIANG

會計　　　杨霞
現場會計　張晔

劇務　　　劉軍
　　　　　沈斌
　　　　　張瑗
　　　　　柏樹君
辦公室助理　李凌云
製片實習　　楊樂樂
湯唯助理　　朱丹
車輛安排　　丁強

上海史實顧問　沈寂
美術顧問　　李寶林

馬來西亞工作人員
策劃

製片（香港）
劇務（香港）
會計（香港）

製作行政
製片
劇務
辦公室聯絡

Production Accountant	YANG XIA
On Set Accountant	ZHANG YE
Production Assistants	LIU JUN
	SHEN BIN
	ZHANG YUAN
	BO SHU JUN
Production Secretary	LI LING YUN
Production Intern	MAX YANG LE LE
Assistant to Tang Wei	ZHU DAN
Tranportation Coordinator	DING QIANG
Shanghai History Consultant	SHEN JI
Art Department Consultant	LEE PAO LIN

MALAYSIA UNIT

Associate Producer (Real Films)	STACEE LAU
Production Manager from HK	ERIC FONG
Unit Manager from HK	WONG KAM MING
Accountant from HK	ROGER LAU
Production Administrator	EVELYN LAU
Production Manager	YEN SAN MICHELLE LO
Unit Manager	MEI NG
Production Coordinators	ALVIN TAN
	LEE CHUNG MING

車輛安排
第二副導演

演員聯絡

外聯製片（檳城）
外聯聯絡（檳城）
外聯製片（怡保）
外聯聯絡（怡保）

助理美術
道具領班

美術部聯絡
美術木工/電工
置景
置景助理
髮型助理

化妝助理
服裝助理

機工

現場收音

選角

Unit/Transport Coordinator	LOOI ZUAN HENG
2nd AD	CHARLOTTE LIM LAY KUEN
	DAVID LOW
Talent Coordinator	YIP YUEN WAI

Location Manager (Penang)	BERT AW
Location Coordinator (Penang)	KOE GAIK CHENG
Location Manager (Ipoh)	GOH WAI FOO
Location Coordinator (Ipoh)	OH KAR YEE

Asst Art Director	KEK TING LAM
Prop Master	WONG VOON LEONG
	MAK HON HUNG
Art Dept Coordinator	CHEN YOKE PIN
Art Dept Carpenter/Electrician	MOHAN SINGH
Location Dresser	CHIAM TAT SIANT
Asst Location Dresser	MAT
Hair Stylist Assts	BELINDA TAN BENNY LIM
	TRACY SIM FION LEE
Make-up Artist Asst	KAREN TAN
Wardrobe Assts	WING SHUM SOT CHENG

Grips	VINCENT CHAI GAN SIONG KING
	WONG SENG NAM TIN KOK YOE
	WONG KIM LOONG YAP KIEN WAI
	YAP GEE YUEN
Additional Prod Sound	GUO LI QI
	VINCENT PHANG
	ALEX THONG

Casting	VICKY LIM LOO LEE

和服提供

髮型助理　西口　久美子
和服助理　相磯　彩美
和服助理　今井　夏子
三昧線老師　堅田　喜三代
藝妓舞蹈老師　中村　繭古
日本選角　西本　龍治
選角助理　笹嶋　和人
選角助理　今村　惠理香
日本聯絡　侯傑輝

後期製作
後期製作行政
第一助理剪接
後期製作助理

聲音剪接主任/對白剪接

音效監製

音效剪接

背景聲音剪接主任
第一背景聲音剪接
背景聲音剪接
第一助理聲音剪接
助理音效剪接

混音

Kimono Sponsor	YAMANO HOLDING GROUP
	KYOUNOKIMONO SIKUNNSI
Katuraya Assistant	NISHIGUCHI KUMIKO
Kimono Kituke	AISO AYAMI
Kimono Kituke	IMAI NATUKO
Syamisenn Teacher	KATADA KIMIYO
Geisha Dance Teacher	NAKAMURA MAYUKO
Casting in Japan	NISHIMOTO RYUJI
Casting Assistant	SASAJIMA KAZUTO
Casting Assistant	IMAMURA ERIKA
Japan Coordinator	CHARLIE HAU

POST PRODUCTION

Post Production Supervisior	GERRY ROBERT BYRNE
First Assistant Editor	GARY LEVY
Post Production Assistant	CALEB WISDORF
Supervising Sound Editor/ Dial Editor	PHILIP STOCKTON
Sound Supervisor/ Sound Designer	EUGENE GEARTY
FX Editor	WYATT SPRAGUE
	MARK FILIP
Foley Supervisor	FRANK KERN
First Foley Editor	STEVEN VISSCHER
Foley Editor	REUBEN SIMON
First Assistant Sound Editor	CHRIS FIELDER
FX Assistant Editor	LARRY WINELAND
Re-recording Mixer	REILLY STEELE

對白重錄剪接主任
對白重錄執行
對白重錄執行
對白重錄語言顧問　　**錢孝貞**
聲音剪接室助理
聲音剪接實習生
背景聲音製作
背景聲音錄製

視覺特效公司
視覺特效主任
視覺特效製作
電腦繪圖主任
數字化監製
數字化繪圖

成影

成影助理

ADR Supervisor	JANE McCULLEY
ADR Assistant Editor	ROLAND VAJS
ADR Assistant/Translator	BETTY TENG
ADR Language Consultant	JEAN TSIEN
Apprentice Sound Editor	JESSICA PARKS
Sound Intern	WILLIAM CHU
Foley Artist	MARKO COSTANZO
Foley Mixer	GEORGE LARA
Special Visual Effects	MR. X, INC.
Visual Effects Supervisor	BRENDAN TAYLOR
Visual Effects Producer	FIONA CAMPBELL WESTGATE
CG Supervisor	WOJCIECH ZIELINSKI
Digital Producer	SARAH McMURDO
Digital Matte Painting	JIM MAXWELL
	MATT SCHOFIELD
Compositing Leads	AARON BARCLAY
	KEVIN QUATMAN
Compositors	MIKE BECKI
	BARB BENOIT
	KRISTY BLACKWELL
	JASON CHAN
	OVIDIU CINAZAN
	ROB DEL CIANCIO
	OMAR GUDJONSSON
	ANNU GULATI
	TIMO HUBER
	MIKLOS KOZARY
	PHILLIP LANGE

成影助理

動畫主管
動畫製作

資深技術主管
特效動畫
燈光

模型材料設計

視覺特效行政
視覺特效監製
工作室管理
製作助理

	EDWARD LEE
	TAMARA STONE
	DAVID THOMPSON
	JEAN PHILIP TRAORE
	ARMANDO VELASQUEZ
	AARON WEINTRAUB
Compositing Assistants	ANAND DORAIRAJ
	VISHAL RUSTGI
	CAROLYN SHELBY
Animation Supervisor	DANIEL MIZUGUCHI
Animation and tracking	DAN CARNEGIE
	HUBERT CHAN
	JASON EDWARDH
	MICHAEL MULOCK
	MATT RALPH
	GAVIN SOARES
	JIM SU
Senior Technical Supervisor	BEN SIMONS
Effects Animation	KYLE YONEDA
Lighting	DOMINIC REMANE
	MANDY AU
Model & Texture Artists	FRED CHU
	MAI-LING LEE
	SEAN MILLS
Visual Effects Coordinator	SARAH BARBER
Visual Effects Executive Producer	DENNIS BERARDI
Studio Operations	DIANA PAZZANO
Production Assistants	MATT GLOVER
	AISHA MALIK

系統管理

美國焦點影業後期製作監制

影片完成擔保

法律顧問

影片製作保險

底片剪接
工作人員薪資服務
銀行服務
後期音效
後期混音
片頭片尾製作

<u>導演鳴謝</u>
鄭培凱
潘迪華
李嘉茜
杜威
韓培珠
盧太
李我
張信剛
陳香梅

Systems Administration	DAVID FIX
	CHRIS NGUYEN
Focus Features Excutive in Charge of Post Production	JEFF ROTH
Completion Guaranty Provided through	CINEFINANCE
Legal Services Provided by	IRA SCHRECK, Esq. &
	JOSEPH DAPELLO, Esq.
	SCHRECK ROSE DAPELLO
	ADAMS & HURWITZ LLP
Insurance	ACORDIA OF CALIFORNIA
	INSURANCE SERVICES, INC.
Negative Cutter	EXACTCUT, TOM MAYCLIM
Payroll Service	ENTERTAINMENT PARTNERS
Banking Service	HSBC BANK USA
Post Production Sound Effects	C5, INC
Post Production Mixing	SOUND ONE CORP.
Titles and End Credits by	YU & CO.

DIRECTOR'S SPECIAL THANKS

PEI-KAI CHENG
REBECCA PAN
JESSIE LEE
FRANKIE TO
HAN POU CHU
MRS. LO
LI NGAW
HSIN-KANG CHANG
ANNA CHAN CHENNAULT

陳溥漢
羅北安
賴聲川
周龍章
陳靜葦

香港鳴謝
香港入境事務處
影視及娛樂事務管理處
娛樂特別效果發牌監督
槍械牌照組
警察公共關係科
香港特別行政區政府
路政署路燈部
路政署
產業署
東區地政署
西貢地政署
海事處
漁農自然護理署
香港郵政
香港大學教務處
香港大學物業處
禹銘投資有限公司（寶珊道）
香港老爺車會
香港歷史博物館
香港淺水灣酒店

P.H. CHAN
LO PEI ON
STAN LAI
ALLEN CHOW
CHENG JING WEI
GUSTAVO SANTAOLALLA

Special thanks to CARTIER for providing
the pink diamond ring

SPECIAL THANKS (Hong Kong)

Hong Kong Immigration Department
Television and Entertainment Licensing Authority
Entertainment Special Effects Licensing Authority
Hong Kong Police Arms Licensing Section
Police Public Relations Branch (PPRB)
Government of the HKSAR
The Lighting Division of Highways Department
Highways Department
Government Property Agency (GPA)
Lands Department District Lands Office—Hong Kong East
Lands Department District Lands Office—Sai Kung
Marine Department
Agriculture, Fisheries and Conservation Department
Hong Kong Post
The University of Hong Kong—The Registry
The University of Hong Kong—Estates Office
Yu Ming Investments Limited
Classic Car Club of Hong Kong (1989) Ltd.
Hong Kong Museum of History
The Repulse Bay Hong Kong

邵氏製片廠
拔萃男書院
東方航空公司
馬來西亞航空公司

<u>上海鳴謝</u>
薛沛建先生
上海文化廣播影視集團
上海電影集團
上海電影製片廠
沈寂先生
上海松江开元名都大酒店
AFFA亲密925银饰专卖店
上海共荣工贸发展有限公司
天安(中国)投资有限公司
上海新場古鎮建設開發有限公司

<u>馬來西亞鳴謝</u>

Shaw Studios
Diocesan Boy's School
China Eastern Airlines Hong Kong Business Office
Malaysia Airlines
Louis Vuitton
Opalus
Cinerent
Tai Fung Supply Fuji Film
Cinelease Inc.

SPECIAL THANKS (Shanghai)
XUE PEI JIAN
Shanghai Media & Entertainment Group
Shanghai Film Group Corporation
Shanghai Film Studio
SHEN JI
Songjiang New Century Grand Hotel Shanghai
AFFA (Affinity) Jewelry
The Goal Company
Tian An China Investment Co., Ltd
Shanghai Xin Chang Town Construction & Development Co., Ltd.

SPECIAL THANKS (Malaysia)
Chief Minister's Office, Penang
Royal Malaysian Police, Penang
Penang Municipal Council
Royal Malaysian Customs, Penang
Tanjung Marina Management Sdn Bhd
Wawasan Open University
Royal Malaysia Police, Ipoh

Ipoh Municipal Council
Fire and Rescue Department Ipoh
Kementerian Kebudayaan, Kesenian dan Warisan

版權屬於 海上影業有限公司